BUILDING
PARENT
TEACHER
COMMUNICATION

AN EDUCATOR'S GUIDE

Cindy J. Christopher

TECHNOMIC
PUBLISHING CO., INC.
LANCASTER · BASEL

BUILDING PARENT-TEACHER COMMUNICATION
a **TECHNOMIC**®publication

Published in the Western Hemisphere by
Technomic Publishing Company, Inc.
851 New Holland Avenue, Box 3535
Lancaster, Pennsylvania 17604 U.S.A.

Distributed in the Rest of the World by
Technomic Publishing AG
Missionsstrasse 44
CH-4055 Basel, Switzerland

Printed in the United States of America
10 9 8 7 6 5 4 3 2 1

Main entry under title:
    Building Parent-Teacher Communication: An Educator's Guide

A Technomic Publishing Company book
Bibliography: p.
Includes index p. 141

Library of Congress Catalog Card No. 95-62130
ISBN No. 1-56676-380-0

BUILDING PARENT-TEACHER COMMUNICATION

HOW TO ORDER THIS BOOK

BY PHONE: 800-233-9936 or 717-291-5609, 8AM–5PM Eastern Time

BY FAX: 717-295-4538

BY MAIL: Order Department
Technomic Publishing Company, Inc.
851 New Holland Avenue, Box 3535
Lancaster, PA 17604, U.S.A.

BY CREDIT CARD: American Express, VISA, MasterCard

BY WWW SITE: http://www.techpub.com

To the Lord, who gave me the precious gift of working with children, and then blessed me with the gift to write; also to my nephew, Drew Christopher, who changed my life in so many wonderful ways.

CONTENTS

FROM THE TIME I entered kindergarten in the 1960s I only wanted one thing and that was to be a teacher. I sought every opportunity I could to work with children and by the time I entered college in my hometown in upstate New York, I was already way ahead of my classmates, many of whom had never worked with children.

I graduated in 1980 and opened a nursery school that I spent seven years directing and in which I taught. It was during that time my love and passion for working with parents began to surface. I developed a rapport with the parents and enjoyed involving them in my curriculum.

One of the hardest things about teaching nursery school was, once the children left to enter elementary school, I lost touch with them. So when the opportunity arose to teach third grade at a rural, central New York school, I grabbed it.

I loved teaching third grade but felt a void because I didn't have daily contact with parents. I then began searching for books on working with parents but could not find any. Over the next seven years I devoted myself to developing and incorporating ways to work with parents as well as getting them interested and involved in what was happening in my classroom.

When conducting workshops for colleges and teaching centers or meeting fellow teachers, I kept track of successful programs, techniques, and problems encountered with parents.

In 1994 I expressed an interest to Technomic about writing another book and was sent a list of suggestions, among which was the topic of working with parents.

I was then off and writing. My goal became the need to develop a handbook of beneficial and relevant ideas, techniques, and solutions to problems that occur when working with parents. I wanted this book to be a resource that teachers in training, new teachers as well as veterans, and administrators could use. As a teacher, I knew it was important to keep this handbook precise and short enough to be read quickly and kept handy for use as a reference guide.

ACKNOWLEDGEMENT

I OWE MANY people a big "thank you," from all the teachers and administrators who supplied information, to proofreader, Charlotte King, who, despite a hectic life-style, always found time to read and reread the manuscript; to my sister-in-law, Cathy, who sent faxes and found phone numbers; to my grandfather for teaching me that writing can bring people and ideas together in spite of long distances; and finally to my mom, Jane, who continues to encourage me to excel and never stop believing that something bigger and brighter comes to those who seek life's best.

I thank each and every one of you. "Commit to the Lord whatever you do, and your plans will succeed" (Proverbs 16:3–NIV).

AS TEACHERS, WE are prepared in undergraduate classes to work with students, but an area often overlooked is working with parents. Research shows that children who succeed have parents who take an interest in their children and schools. If children know their parents believe school is important in order to succeed, they also place importance in it. Our job becomes much easier when this happens.

The problem is how do teachers get parents interested and involved? How do we keep them informed? How do we handle problems that arise? How can we get over feeling intimidated? How can we, as teachers, protect ourselves through documentation? What techniques work? How do we have successful parent-teacher conferences? How can we let parents know what their child's strengths and weaknesses are?

This handbook is written to provide answers to questions such as these plus cover the wide range of areas encompassed in working with parents. Over the course of fourteen years, material was gathered from fellow teachers, administrators, workshops I have conducted and attended, questionnaires, and parent feedback. Information was compiled into sections concerning contact before school, informing and involving parents, documentation, assessment, problems frequently encountered, and tips.

Contained in these pages, you will find actual strategies and proven examples already in place in schools throughout the country. You will be led, step-by-step, through the stages of successfully making the first-time contact with parents as well as the importance of involving parents by using teacher-proven methods

xiii

that will make you excited and eager to implement them in your classroom.

Also included is the "how and why" of documentation concerning anecdotal, student classwork, parent notes, and conferences. You will experience some of the new types of assessment and the benefits parents gain from them.

Working with parents can be tough and sometimes exhausting. It can be nerve-wracking, and there are some parents you can never reach or make happy no matter what you do. Despite the problems, there are many benefits of parents and teachers working together outlined in this handbook. Education consists of one-third teacher, one-third parent, one-third student and when all three sides work together, the result is a stronger educational system and a successful child.

By the time you finish reading this handbook, hopefully you will be excited and "on fire" to make parents vital parts of your program. You may choose to involve, or only to inform the parents, but you can be positive that whatever you do, the benefits will be long-lasting. You can be encouraged and supported in linking and working with the parents of the children you see everyday.

Good luck as you embark on a wonderful journey reaching out to parents who can help you become a more effective and dynamic educator.

CHAPTER 1

Parent Communication Before School Begins

AS THE END of a school year approaches, teachers begin year-end tests, finish updating cumulative folders, and straighten out their rooms. In most instances teachers do not think about communicating with the parents of the students they will teach in the fall. The emphasis is on just getting through the chaos at the end of a school year.

However, if time is taken to communicate with parents in some manner, the transition for incoming students seems to be smoother. Parents are more informed about what the expectations are and what materials are needed. This helps everyone with the adjustment to a new grade level. Parents appreciate the extra time put forth and most are willing to establish a positive rapport with teachers even before their child has entered school in the fall.

This chapter will offer some examples of ways to communicate with incoming parents. Remember, when parents are informed, the result is a stronger and more effective educational structure.

WAYS TO COMMUNICATE BEFORE SCHOOL STARTS

Orientation Night

One group of sixth-grade teachers holds an orientation night in May for parents of fifth-grade students who will be in sixth grade in the fall. Each teacher presents a curriculum, gives an overview of expectations, homework, discipline, materials needed, and so on. They also have handouts available for the parents to take home. This way parents are aware of what is expected of them and their child the following year. This format is repeated in the fall for parents who couldn't attend or parents new to the district. Parents who came to the orientation in the spring also attend in the fall to reverify and/or find out any additional information.

Orientation nights are very popular in many junior and senior high schools where transitions from one school to another or changing of classes occurs.

Informative Letter

On the very last day of school, many districts have a "moving up" day in which children meet their next year's teacher. Many teachers use this opportunity to give each child a packet of information to take home that pertains to the classroom. In the packet is a letter to parents (Figure 1a) that may cover the following areas:

- how to help children over the summer in math, reading, and writing
- items needed for the next grade
- clothing needed for recess
- other tidbits of information
- how parents can become involved in the classroom
- expectations for the upcoming year
- brief overview or highlights of curriculum
- classroom policies

By sending the letter home in June, parents have the opportunity to learn about requirements and the theory of how the classroom is run.

Also, on the first day of school most children come with the appropriate items, and parents don't need to go out that first week and fight the back-to-school crowds. Parents on limited incomes or budgets can take advantage of early back-to-school sales throughout the summer. Teachers who give students a list of things they need that first week of school often find students' parents have already bought school items and many times they are not what you have on the list. This eliminates the guesswork.

Dear Parent(s),

I am very happy to have your child in my classroom and look forward to an exciting 1995–1996 school year. I run my room based on love, respect, and caring. We are a family for a year and must learn to get along with one another.

I believe in order for parents to assume an active role in their child's education, they must be kept informed of what is happening in the classroom. Each Friday I send out newsletters in large manila envelopes that are returned and reused. Newsletters contain information about special events or things happening in the room, plus a weekly diary of everything that has been taught. A monthly calendar listing spelling words, specials, cursive letters taught, birthdays, due dates for projects, and any other pertinent information is sent home at the beginning of each month.

If you would like to volunteer for classroom activities, you are in the right room! I plan many special activities and can use all the help I can get. Without help the "extras" can't happen. I also use "room moms or dads" (responsible for planning parties, helping in room, or any other classroom needs), and if you have the time to assume any of these responsibilities, let me know in September.

Every morning your child may bring in something for a quick snack that can be consumed in fifteen minutes. (NO CANDY OR JUNK FOOD ALLOWED!) For forty cents students may purchase milk. I have a small refrigerator in my room for storage of juice boxes or things that need to be kept cold. If you wish to celebrate your child's birthday in school, please make arrangements with me in advance. If you would like to send in snacks for the class, please feel free to do so. (Chocolate-chip cookies are my favorites!)

Third grade is a tough transition for students due to many new concepts and skills being taught. Students learn the computer keyboard in third grade. I use parent volunteers to help watch and teach the appropriate keys to students at the computer. If you have an hour and are interested in helping out, let me know. Students in my room often learn almost the entire keyboard because of the help that comes from parents. Because computer technology in our school is thought to be one of the best in the state, learning the keyboard allows students to focus entirely on the programs.

Multiplication, division, and cursive writing are introduced, and grades are now given for english, social studies, and science. To help with this, I strongly urge you to work with addition and subtraction flashcards and have your child read at least fifteen minutes a day. Buy a spiral notebook and have your child write an entry each day about what they did that day. You will be surprised at the difference it can make in adjustment. If your child had problems or failed any academic areas in second grade, they should be worked on during the summer. Problem areas left unattended only get worse.

Students go outside for recess every day (weather and wind chill cooperating) and should come dressed accordingly. During winter students must wear snow pants or a snowsuit, boots, gloves, and a hat. If they don't they will not be allowed to go out and will have detention in the room.

There will be a short homework assignment on Monday and Wednesday nights. It will help students become responsible for doing work at home and returning it to school. Any work not completed in school must be taken home and returned, completed, the next day. You may check the Homework Hotline, which is a useful tool to keep you informed of what is happening in the classroom.

Figure 1a *Letter to parents.*

Your child will need the following items the first day of school:

- loose-leaf paper (Please buy regular ruled paper, not college ruled, because it is too small and leads to messy handwriting.)
- 2 packages of #2 pencils
- crayons and crayon box
- 2 pocket folders (make sure the pocket is long enough to hold papers so they won't fall out)
- 2 folders with three brass fasteners on the inside that will hold notebook paper
- glue stick, ruler, pair of scissors

As these supplies run out, you are responsible for replenishing them throughout the year.

I look forward to meeting and working with each one of you! Have a nice and relaxing summer. I will see you in the fall. Do not hesitate to call me if you have any questions. As you will learn, my door is always open to you. By working together we can provide the best learning experiences for your child!

Please take the time to fill out the enclosed Parent Questionnaire, and have your child fill out the Student Questionnaire. Return them to me as quickly as possible. This will help me better prepare and meet the needs of ALL of my students.

Sincerely,

Teacher's name

Figure 1a (continued) *Letter to parents.*

Questionnaires

Also included in the packet are two questionnaires, one for parents (see Figure 1b), and the other for the student to fill out (see Figure 1c) and return before school starts.

When completed, the parent and student questionnaires allow the teacher to have advanced insight into the strengths/weaknesses and interests of incoming students. Activities, curriculum, and learning centers can be geared to meet the needs of the incoming class. Parents and students realize their opinions are valued and that the teacher cares enough to ask them questions. If questionnaires are not returned, the teacher will know which parents need to be contacted in order to draw them into the classroom.

Home Visits

Another way to meet students and parents in a nonthreatening way is to make home visits over the summer. Call each parent in advance and set up a time to stop by, say hello, and become acquainted. You can learn a lot about each family by observing them in their home environment.

A word of caution—make sure when setting up home visits that parents understand that you want to get to know each family personally and you would like them to do the same with you. Emphasize that you are not coming to judge them.

Many teachers enjoy home visits as a way to meet families because they get to know the interests and makeup of each home.

End-of-the-Summer Picnic

Depending on the type of district you teach in, home visits may not be well-received. Plan an end-of-the-summer picnic at a park, the school playground, the beach, or wherever you can get people together. Have each family bring meat and a dish to share to pass around. Plan activities that involve family participation. Some of the teachers I spoke with love to use this method because students get to meet their classmates and relieve some of those beginning-day jitters about making new friends. Also, instead of

Parent Questionnaire

Directions: Please complete the following questions to help me better meet the needs of your child.

Academic

1. What are your child's strongest areas?

2. What are your child's weakest areas?

3. Has your child received any help for academics outside of the classroom? If so, in what areas?

4. What are three academic goals you would like to see your child achieve in this grade?

5. Do you have any other pertinent information you wish to share that may help me in assessing your child's academics?

Emotional

1. Does your child have any emotional needs that may interfere with learning? I need to be aware of that.

2. Has there been any significant change that might have brought on emotional stress (such as, death, moving, divorce)?

3. In the past has your child seen the school counselor or psychologist for emotional problems?

Social

1. List your child's strongest social skill.

2. Does your child need help in a social area? If so, what area? Has anything been done to help your child in this area prior to this grade?

3. Do you have any long-term social goals you would like your child to accomplish this year?

Figure 1b Parent questionnaire.

Physical

1. What is your child's strongest area?

2. What is your child's weakest area?

3. In what kinds of physical activities does your child express an interest?

4. Does your child have any special physical needs?

If there is anything else I should know before I meet your child, please feel free to write a note in the space provided.

Figure 1b (continued) Parent questionnaire.

Student Questionnaire

Directions: Please complete the following statements with the first thing that comes to mind.

1. The best thing about school is . . .

2. The worst thing about school is . . .

3. The subject that is hardest is . . .

4. The subject that is easiest is . . .

5. I hope this year I can learn about . . .

6. I would like to improve in . . .

7. The best thing about last year's teacher was . . .

8. I want my new teacher to . . .

9. List anything you are interested in or would like to learn about below.

Figure 1c Student questionnaire.

spending a month meeting each family, you can do it in an afternoon.

The new multiage program in Tully, New York, had a picnic the week before school started and families were invited to meet one another, their teachers, and visit the classrooms. This picnic was so well-received that it will become a yearly activity. The teachers of this program felt this positive, nonthreatening way of meeting families opened the door of communication between parents and teachers. The parents did not have to wait until the school had an open house before they were invited for a visit. They were able to see the classroom and meet the teacher, putting them on a common ground with their child. The interest level in starting the school year was high because parents felt they were actually being encouraged to participate.

Postcards

Some teachers send out postcards to the parents and students with a note welcoming them to the grade level and mentioning the items needed for the first day.

Letter Home during the Last Week of Vacation

Mail a note to parents similar to the one found in Figure 1a. Include the following information:

- Welcome parents as part of the team (one-third teacher, one-third parent, one-third student equals success).
- Briefly tell about your professional background. Include hobbies and interests so parents will see you, not only as a teacher, but a person with outside interests. It also allows parents to discuss common interests.
- Explain teaching philosophy and style of teaching.
- Give the daily schedule.
- List the books used.
- If homework is given, state expectations.
- Describe discipline expectations and consequences.
- Give home phone number.

I realize giving home phone numbers makes some teachers very uncomfortable. Sometimes to have parents call the teacher at home and not wait until a problem escalates into a major one solves almost every problem before it reaches the catastrophic stage.

I also encourage parents to call me by my first name. Some teachers disagree with this because they see it as unprofessional. I feel that being on a first-name basis with me is much more personal and friendly. Some parents will prefer to address teachers as Mrs., Mr., or Miss because they see a teacher as a person in authority. Much of this reflects leftover negative feelings parents still carry around concerning their own school experience.

A letter sent home allows parents and students to have a clear picture of what is expected. Communication lines have been established without even meeting the parents.

Phone Call

Call each parent prior to the first day of school to introduce yourself. This gives you the opportunity to welcome parents and answer any questions they may have.

GUIDELINES FOR CONTACT

(1) Depending on the grade level you teach, your objective for contact will be different. A first-grade teacher needs to develop a different rapport with parents due to the inability of students to communicate effectively, whereas a tenth-grade teacher would find an orientation night more relevant.

(2) Keep the contact simple and positive. It is okay to let parents know your feelings and opinions, but you don't need to go overboard or into too much detail.

(3) Not all parents will be friendly or willing to come to a school function. Some may be embarrassed because of their appearance, by their wealth, or lack of it, and their own personal feelings concerning school. Just keep on trying to inform them and you may be surprised at the change by the end of the year. Personal invitations do make a difference.

The major goal throughout this chapter is that an effort is being made to "touch base" with parents before the beginning of a new school year. There is no better way to start a school year than knowing that parents have been made to feel welcome and informed. You also have a general feeling for the network of parents and you can better relate to each one.

CHAPTER 2

Informing Parents

FOR MANY TEACHERS, working with parents is the toughest part of teaching. Some teachers are easily intimidated by parents because they feel they are constantly being judged. Teachers have to keep in mind that perhaps as many as half of the parents had a less than successful experience as children in school, which has carried over to how they view their child's school experience. Walking into schools can make some parents feel as if they were right back in school themselves. They become uneasy, sometimes quick to judge, and attack out of a feeling of inferiority.

You, as the teacher, must find a means to make them feel welcome, comfortable, involved, and informed. Research shows that children who succeed in school have parents who take an interest in their children and the school they attend. By easing parents' fear of school, one sees them eventually joining parent groups, attending academic meetings, or calling school to inquire about problems. Children learn better when parents and teachers are working together toward the same goal, their success!

Administrators, when surveyed, said the most frequent complaint they received from parents concerning teachers was the feeling that teachers were not understanding, were inflexible or mean, and did not encourage communication. These teachers with a problem would call parents and in many cases dump the problem into the parents' laps, instead of offering to work together toward a solution. These are the teachers who have severe problems dealing with the children who don't fit into that nice, neat, "great student" mold. They are unable to find methods to meet the needs of *all* of their students and deal accordingly with the parents.

Administrators often find that the communication problem results from parents and teachers not asking the right question or questions. One story shared with me was about a kindergarten child, who, when asked by his mom about snack milk, said he wasn't getting any. She called the school, extremely upset, because she had been sending milk money and her son stated he had not received any milk snack. The truth was that the children were not receiving milk, but juice. A funny story, but how realistic. When you think about problems that occur in the classroom, many could be lumped under the heading of miscommunication.

Throughout the seven years I directed and taught nursery school, the number-one complaint parents had with public or private education was their lack of knowledge as to what was happening in their child's classroom. When they would ask their child about what happened in school, the usual response was, "Nothing." When I accepted a position to teach third grade, I vowed that none of the parents of my students would ever be able to say they weren't informed.

I work hard to keep parents abreast of classroom happenings. When parents are kept informed, they become your biggest supporters and are very vocal. Each year I get numerous phone calls and letters from parents thanking me for making them feel they are active participants in their child's school year.

However, I am alarmed at the number of teachers who state they are either too busy keeping up with the day-to-day demands of teaching or they do not see a need to keep parents informed. Some teachers believe we get paid to teach children, not to work with parents. I wonder what would happen to the educational system in this country if every teacher informed parents what was happening and being taught in the classroom.

As a parent, how can you work with your child(ren) if you don't even know what is being taught. Some of you reading this might say, well, parents could look over their child's papers. I have had parents tell me that some teachers don't even pass papers back to students. These students have no idea how good or bad they are doing until report cards are out. Sometimes it is not the fault of teachers, but the fault of the student who put work in the trash can without the teacher or the parents knowing it.

I am a very strong advocate for parents and believe informing and involving parents is an area widely overlooked. Teachers are taught strategies that work with children but not to deal effectively with parents. When parents are involved and informed, working with the teacher and not against, the result is a better educational experience for children. Very few parents are unreachable, but it takes time to find the right approach to keep them informed and excited about what is happening in the classroom. Don't let anyone ever tell you that parents don't want to be involved. They do! They often just don't know how.

Teachers who keep parents informed find that parents are more apt to be supportive in dealing with classroom problems involving their child, and are willing to work with the teacher in finding solutions. These parents are more likely to volunteer for special activities and are more content because they know what is happening. When they have questions or concerns, they are more willing to pick up the phone and call the teacher. When parents know the "hows," "whys," "whats" of how a classroom is managed, most negative encounters are diverted.

Throughout this chapter are a variety of ways to keep parents informed and interested from nursery school through twelfth grade. Find a method that works for you and you will be amazed at the difference it makes. A word of caution—no matter what method you choose, remember there will always be parents you won't be able to please. Don't let that stand in the way of those that you can reach.

NEWSLETTERS

Newsletters are the number-one way to reach all parents on a regular basis. Yet many teachers do not take advantage of this wonderful communication opportunity. Newsletters may be done in a variety of ways with no one method being superior to another. The purpose is to communicate between school and home what is taking place in the classroom. Find a method that will work best for you and meet your objectives.

TYPES OF NEWSLETTERS

Student-Directed Newspaper

On Fridays the children write a couple of sentences about each subject stating things they have learned throughout the week. This paper is taken home.

Class Newspaper

A class newspaper works well in the upper grades where students can be put in charge of gathering information, meeting deadlines, and collating. Choose two students as editors who can assign "stories." Make sure deadlines are kept and that the paper comes out on time. The teacher can give "an article" to students to include in the newspaper.

I tried this technique and found that the results were amazing. The editorials had much thought behind them and proved that students, when given a chance, have valuable suggestions and opinions.

Journals

Children can either write daily or once a week to parents informing them about what they have been doing in school. They take the journal home once a week and the parents enter a quick reply.

This works best with children, third grade or above, or with advanced students in the lower grades. It is important for parents to know in advance what you expect their obligation to be. Stress you are looking for positive feedback!

Class-Directed Newspaper

The teacher sits down with the class and they compose the newsletter together. At the end of the day in Joan Osborne's first-grade class, they sit on the rug and discuss what happened that day. They move from discussion time to writing a couple of sentences, such as, "We had music outside. It's red and black day. It's hot out." This method is great for the lower grades where the students are too young to write or in grades where teachers are introducing the writing process.

Teacher-Directed Newspaper

This type of newsletter is one in which the teacher does the writing. This is the method I use for the sake of convenience. My schedule is so tight that I find it easier to do myself (see Figures 2a and 2b for an example).

CONTENTS OF NEWSLETTERS

Nonacademic Information

Nonacademic information may include such things as upcoming deadlines of assignments or projects, test dates, birthdays, assemblies, activities, announcements, news about what is going on in the classroom and in the school, and things for which you would like parent help (Figure 2a).

Academic Areas

I find it very important for parents to be made aware of what skills and concepts are being taught. Some parents like to help their child at home or discuss things being taught. As discussed before, most children, when asked what they learned in school,

---

May 5, 1995

Dear Parents,

Please bring your child to the gym at 6:50 P.M. next Wednesday in order to help set up for the science fair. All science experiment sheets should have been returned so final copies can be done.

Anyone interested in sewing the batting in the quilt please let me know.

Thanks for all the help on the cooking project. Everyone had a great time preparing and eating!

Book reports due next Thursday.

Please return report-card envelopes promptly.

Figure 2a Nonacademic portion of newsletter.

Reading—We are finishing up the book *Sarah, Plain and Tall* and we will be seeing the movie next week. Ask us what we liked best about the book, who the characters were, where the story took place, and what we learned about Sarah.

Spelling—We all had individualized lists this week because it was a review unit. Some of us need to take our studying more seriously. We can do that by practicing more.

Short Stuff—We finished the sentence starters to . . .

The best thing I did on vacation was . . .

In fourth grade I hope . . .

Social Studies—We are working very hard building our communities. Models will be on display at our talent night.

Science—We are learning about electricity. Ask us the following questions:

- What are the three parts of a flashlight?
- What are some ways we can conserve around the house?
- How does an electromagnet work?
- What are three ways we use electric motors?
- Electricity gives off two types of energy. What are they?
- What does the thickness of the wire have to do with the amount of heat and light produced when electricity passes through it?

If we don't know these answers, we either need to pay better attention and/or study more. Test next Wednesday.

Cursive—We learned the lower case letters *w, x,* and *v*. Now we can do all the lower case letters. Next week—start upper case.

Math—We are working on identifying and writing fractions, plus changing improper fractions into mixed numbers. (Example 20/3 means 20 divided by 3 which equals 6 and 2/3.) Please help us at home changing whole fractions into mixed ones because some of us are confused. It's also great practice for long division.

Journal—Entries included: *My Home, My Favorite Season, My Favorite Birthday*. Have a great weekend! Hopefully warm weather will begin drifting our way soon!

Figure 2b *Academic portion of newsletter.*

reply they have done nothing. By keeping parents informed of skills and concepts, parents have the background to discuss school with their child.

In my newsletters I list each academic area and briefly state in two or three sentences what skills or concepts were taught throughout the week (Figure 2b). If new skills will be introduced the next week, I let parents know in advance.

For example, under the heading of math, a parent might read, "We are finishing with the concept of multiplication. Each child should be able to explain and draw the concept of multiplication. (Four times two means four groups of two things in each group.) Now is the time to dig out the multiplication flash cards and begin drilling them at home."

Notice that in Figure 2b I wrote "we" when I started out. It is important for the students to read the newsletter out loud to their parents. By using "we," they will realize "they" are whom the newsletter has been written about. Also, never assume parents know what skills and concepts are being taught because of the parents' wide variety of educational experiences, from those who never finished school to those with doctorate degrees. Therefore, it is important to explain what the concept of multiplication means. If the subject warrants, add things parents can practice at home with their child. In social studies and science, list concepts and questions they can discuss with their child that relate to the subject being taught.

Newsletters are sent home each Friday in manila envelopes that the children return on Monday. This way the teacher knows parents are receiving information.

Other Things to Include in Newsletters

- vocabulary words to be introduced the upcoming week
- A monthly calendar (see Figure 2c for third-grade example) that lists specials, deadlines for projects, spelling words, birthdays, assemblies, and other pertinent information. The monthly calendar is relevant to any grade level and type of information and can be adjusted accordingly. A high-school teacher may choose to list assignment due dates, whereas a kindergarten calendar may be very detailed. Parents love this because they can see weekly

October 95	Monday	Tuesday	Wednesday	Thursday	Friday
few them as grew of so flew come new Bonus: room afternoon food tissue shoe any stew down	2 Music Computer Child of week Jessica	3 Art Kid's Project Assembly- 8:45 a.m.	4 Gym Book orders due	5 Library Music Happy Birthday Carrie	6 No Students
Review unit- each child has individualized lists	9 Columbus Day No School	10 Art Child of week Shane PTO meeting 7:00 p.m.	11 Gym Fire Prevention 10:50-11:10	12 Music Computer Book Reports Due cooking day	13 Art Family Morning 7-8 a.m.
send one yes that keep since book Bonus: us city dress guess can circus soon center seen twice	16 Gym Child of week Richie Student teacher begins	17 Library Music Cursive test	18 Art Happy Birthday Meghan	19 Gym Unit 3 Science Test	20 Music Computer T-shirt + popcorn day
bug go game has rag got huge Bonus: just giant sponge job stranger good danger get page November	23 Art Child of week Amanda	24 Gym Food Project Due	25 Library Music Reading Quarter Test	26 Art Book Reports Due	27 Gym Free Willy 2 at High School 7:00 p.m.
drive my give had dry before time little I try high find just right by Bonus: friend fine Halloween parade	30 Music Computer Child of week Alex	31 Art Halloween party + parade- 1:20	Nov. 1 Gym	2 Library Music Field trip money due	3 Art science experiments- Dan, Matt, Carrie, Kelly

Figure 2c Monthly calendar.

what projects are due as well as the spelling word list to practice. If you are a parent, you know how hard it can be to get your child to bring home a spelling list to study. The calendar alleviates this problem.

- A book entitled, *Letters to Parents*, written by Anthony D. Fredericks and Elaine P. LeBlanc, has forty ready-to-duplicate letters with over 200 ideas for building reading skills at home (published by Good Year Books in Glenview, Illinois). This is a must for every teacher.
- monthly school menu
- schoolwide news coming from the main office
- Always look for articles that have ways parents can increase parenting skills or ways to work with their children at home. Parents will help if they know how to help their child with homework, or work on problems in academic subjects, or to be more effective in their discipline techniques.

OTHER WAYS TO INFORM

Weekly Plans

At the end or beginning of each week, jot parents a letter (no more than a page long) advising them of the plans for the week. If you want to make sure parents receive and have read the letter, have them sign a form. Offer a place for comments. You may be surprised at the resources parents send in that may supplement your subjects. Some parents will offer their help especially in lesson plans that appeal to them. (For example, if you are learning about Germany and a parent has been there or speaks German, they may offer to come in.) It is surprising how many parents want to become involved when they know what is being taught.

Barbara Mallonee, a fifth-grade veteran teacher of twenty-five years, sends home a sheet on Mondays that basically contains her planbook for the week. Her parents are aware of her methods and know to look for the sheet and check to see what is being taught in school.

Parent/Student Signatures Concerning Upcoming Assignments

Mary Ann Murphy, a business-education teacher, makes the parents of seventh-grade students sign a paper that states the assignment requirements of the child and due dates. When the paper is returned, Mary Ann can be sure that the parents are aware of the child's responsibilities. Therefore, if she needs to call parents concerning assignments, there are no surprises.

Along the same lines, when projects are assigned, send home a note concerning the requirements for the project and what is needed for an *A, B,* and so on. This way, when a child does poorly on an assignment, the parent knows in advance what was required (see Chapter 5, the Rubrics section).

Happy Calls

In many cases the only contact that parents and teachers have is when a child is having a discipline or academic problem. Research shows that the first contact with parents should be on a positive note, but many teachers ignore the research. A "happy call" is a great way to give positive feedback to a parent without spending a tremendous amount of time doing it.

A happy call is made on a designated night to a certain number of parents for the sole purpose of informing them of something wonderful their child has done. Some suggestions are listed below that might warrant a phone call:

- Child has mastered some new skill or concept.
- Child always comes to class prepared.
- Child always hands in homework on time.
- Child has had no discipline problems or has improved in this area.
- Child has done extra work beyond what was required.
- Child has displayed some act of kindness to others.

Before beginning happy calls, send home a note explaining that, whatever night you choose, you will be calling four parents with a one- to two-minute phone call. These calls are only for the purpose of giving positive recognition to their child.

Within a five- to six-week period you will have placed calls to every parent and then can start again. You will find parents love these happy calls. What parents don't like to hear something positive about their child?

A kindergarten teacher at Franklin School in Binghamton, New York, places surprise phone calls with "Happy News" to parents during the day. If you don't have time in the evening, a daytime call is just as effective and popular. Choose the style of calling that fits your individual life-style.

Happy Notes

Happy notes are really the same as happy calls except that the teacher writes the note and sends it home. With computers in many classrooms, many teachers love the certificates and notes they can make in a short amount of time. Students are happy to take a note home when they know it contains positive feedback. You can be sure the note will get into a parent's hands.

Periodic Phone Calls

Marty Brophy, a kindergarten teacher, has had much success with phone calls to parents on a periodic basis. He calls each parent monthly and in some cases more than that. In the back of his plan book, he keeps track of each phone call. He quickly tells parents how things are going and then asks them if they have any questions or problems (no matter how small or insignificant they may seem). Many small problems are solved immediately. They will fester if left alone because most parents will not call and ask questions. He finds that when there is a problem, he already has parents in his corner ready to offer help. There is no lack of communication, because he is touching base with parents on a regular monthly schedule. His goal is that, by the end of the year, each parent will feel comfortable enough to contact him first. When they do so, he feels he has completed the steps involved in encouraging an open line of communication.

Homework Hotline

The Syracuse, New York newspapers, along with P&C Foods, offer central New York teachers the use of a program called "Homework Hotline." A teacher who wishes to use this service dials the audiotext system's main number, punches in a code, and records a message one to two minutes long to parents and/or students. Parents can then call this hotline number twenty-four hours a day, seven days a week, punch in the teacher's four-digit code, and listen to the message. Parents who call may hear a summary of learning activities, homework assignments, home learning suggestions, changes in the curriculum, and so on. Students who call may be given bonus assignments worth extra credit.

The success of Homework Hotline has been overwhelming. In a low-income housing project, one-third of the parents call each day. Teachers state this hotline seems to be an effective tool in dealing with at-risk students, reducing the number of school dropouts, improving achievement, and increasing school/community involvement. Parents, who normally would not call teachers because they do not wish to disturb them, do not want to be drawn into long conversations, or do not wish to appear foolish or ignorant, are more likely to call the hotline. Parents who are afraid of school lose this fear within a few weeks due to hearing the teacher's messages. The increased homework completion boosts grades and improves parental communication and participation in schools.

Homework Hotline is a great and very effective tool in communicating with parents, especially at the middle grade levels. Parents have less time than they did years ago, but Homework Hotline involves a phone call and a couple of minutes of listening to a message that keeps parents up-to-date. Over two thousand central New York teachers take advantage of this program, which is free thanks to P&C Foods.

Lesson Line

First Tennessee Bank has developed a free service, similar to Homework Hotline, called Lesson Line. Lesson Line is available to all schools and parents in areas where the bank does business. Currently 800 schools in twenty Tennessee communities are taking advantage of this school-to-home communication link. Teachers record messages for parents regarding what's happening in the classroom: homework assignments, study tips, test schedules, classroom activities, community events and more. Parents can access the messages from any touch-tone phone from 5:00 P.M. until 7:30 A.M. Lesson Line received more than 4 million calls from parents during the 1994–1995 school year. A random survey of parents indicates that 93 percent of the parents who use Lesson Line say it increases their involvement in their child's education. Lesson Line has also been shown to increase parent volunteerism in the schools, raise homework completion rates and students' grades.

Student Information Night

Select a night when students are put in charge of informing parents concerning certain aspects of the curriculum. They may tell about routine, class structure, schedule, grading, homework policy, and so on. The teachers who use this say that, because students are in charge, they put pressure on parents to attend, resulting in the majority of parents attending Information Night.

Journal Notebook

A great way to keep in touch with parents whose children are discipline problems, struggling, or do not complete assignments is to correspond with parents by using a notebook. Parents are kept informed and are expected to also write comments, and/or concerns in the notebook. Many teachers who use this method see positive results because of the constant communication between teacher and parents. When parents are kept informed, they know how to help and will work with the teacher in trying to remedy the problem. This method also works well when documentation is needed. Number the pages so that they can't be ripped out without the parents or teacher noticing that they are missing.

Handbook

Many schools create a handbook for parents that explains general information concerning the school and its policies. Some of the things discussed may be: schedules, student conduct, attendance policy, health information, transportation, report cards, parent-teacher conferences, special areas, grading procedure, and office information. Parents are urged to read through the handbook and save it for future reference.

Pride Board

To help students increase self-esteem and take pride in themselves design a bulletin board entitled "Packed with Pride." In advance discuss with students ways in which they can be proud of the things they do, or accomplish, or even attempt to achieve. Examples may be such things as: Caitlin is proud she knows how to type, Eric is proud he has learned multiplication facts of six to nine, or Shanna is proud she made band. Have colored markers available for students to write responses on the board. Make up a certificate similar to the one in Figure 2d that students complete to take home to display. Encourage parents to make such a board at home for their families. Stress that pride boards help children take an active role in self-recognition of things that they are proud of.

School Calendar

Some districts provide a yearly school calendar for parents and taxpayers within their district. Information such as specific dates for sporting events, college prep tests, kindergarten registration, band and chorus concerts, physicals, field trips, and so on are included. Also contained within the calendar (in place of pictures) are such things as bus routes, qualifications for reduced lunch/breakfast programs, ways to help children at home, how to tell if a child is a substance abuser, etc. These calendars require advance planning on the part of teachers and administrators but are worth the effort because parents are indeed informed.

CONCLUSION

As you have seen throughout this chapter, there are many ways to inform parents. A teacher must select ways that fit the teacher's schedule without overburdening anyone. The suggestions shared throughout this chapter work at all grade levels. So, if you are a junior- or senior-high teacher and think informing parents

PACKED WITH PRIDE

DEAR FAMILY,

I AM PROUD OF

MYSELF BECAUSE

_____

_____

_____

LOVE,

Figure 2d.

is not important in the higher grades, guess again. Elementary and middle grade teachers have traditionally been known to do more to inform parents, while in higher grades, communication begins to go downhill.

With the introduction of computers in classrooms and homes, many teachers find the technological advances help save time. Computers can help with record keeping, phone lists, grading, five-week reports, documentation, and printing and designing documents.

Keeping parents informed is much easier with the many new programs now available. Many teachers love the grading programs because you can get averages at the press of a key, which is extremely beneficial to upper grades where weekly reports may be needed. Parents and students can be kept informed of progress without teachers having to spend a lot of extra time averaging grades. Notes and newsletters are more professional looking and with the grammatical and spell checks computers provide, you don't have to worry as much about spelling or grammatical errors. Some schools even have five-week reports and report-card programs where teachers only have to enter student data and comments.

A word of caution—make sure you save data on two separate disks if you use floppy disks. This way, if a disk is damaged, you have a backup disk.

As technology continues to advance daily, more and more teachers will find programs that help them communicate more effectively with parents. The result is parents who are much more informed and eager to get involved.

CHAPTER 3

Involving Parents

IN THE LAST chapter we looked at ways to inform parents. Once you begin to do this, you may notice parents are more eager to get involved in their child's class activities. This is when some teachers begin to get nervous. Teachers have not been taught how to interact with others. We are basically autonomous in our jobs. When we shut that classroom door, we become the boss. Therefore, when someone wants to enter the classroom, we think of a million excuses not to let the person in.

In order for teachers to involve parents, we must realize we are professionals. Just as we wouldn't walk into a doctor's office and try to run it, parents are not there to judge or criticize us. If a teacher is that uncomfortable, one would have to ask why. Maybe the teacher needs to evaluate his teaching. Is the teacher doing his best job? Is he giving it 100 percent? If so, the fear and the uneasiness need to be dealt with. One way to cope is to begin inviting people who are nonthreatening to visit the classroom. Soon the teacher will be used to seeing another adult in the room and the insecurity will dissolve.

If you squirmed when you read the questions above and suspect you are not doing your best, then it's time to get back on track. Enroll in some teaching courses to get updated on methods and new programs. After teaching the same grade level for a number of years, it could be very easy to step back and relax, but attending workshops can keep you fresh and enthusiastic. Teaching is a profession that is changing continually, and unless you keep up with the new terminology and methods, you could be left in the dark.

TYPES OF SCHOOLWIDE INVOLVEMENT

Back-to-School Night

More and more school districts offer a "Back-to-School Night" for parents to attend without the students. Parents spend between twenty and thirty minutes in their child's classroom, while the teacher goes over expectations and curriculum. A time is usually provided for answering questions from parents.

The district where I teach has done this for a couple of years. Parents and teachers have stated they now prefer the "Back-to-School Night." Parents learn first-hand about expectations and how the teacher operates his/her classroom.

Many teachers hand out a booklet or flyer to each parent. This material contains the learning objectives for the academic area, grading policy, homework policy, purpose of weekly newsletters, routines, upcoming activities scheduled throughout the year, and how they, as parents, fit into the picture. Requirements for book reports, science experiments, and homework tips can also be included. This way parents have a booklet to refer to throughout the school year and can see in September where their child will be by the end of the year.

Open House

Open House gives parents the opportunity to visit the school and their children's classrooms. Usually this is done with the students in attendance. Teachers usually have students' work on display. This is the school's chance to "show off" to parents. Some schools have a Science Fair, Computer Showcase, Book Fair, and so on, to compliment the Open House.

If your school does not permit students to attend with their parents, you may wish to have children copy or fill out a letter (Figure 3a).

National Education Week

This is generally a week in November when parents are invited to visit the classroom during school hours. They get to view first-hand the routine of their child's classroom and the teaching style

Dear

    Thank you for visiting my classroom. Inside my desk please look at. . . . While you are in the classroom, make sure you look at. . . . My favorite subject is . . . because. . . . The best thing about school so far is. . . . Some of my friends' names are. . . .

    If you have time before you leave, would you please write me a quick note to tell me what you thought of my classroom?

Love,

Figure 3a Open House letter.

of the teacher. Have students write a personal invitation to their parents inviting them to come to school. Plan activities in which you can include parents. Have three or four students work in cooperative groups with their parents solving problems.

Shared Decision Making

In many states it is becoming mandatory for parents to be involved in educational reform. For example, under New York State's Compact for Learning, a shared decision team consisting of teachers, parents, administrators, and students work together to increase academic achievement. The emphasis of this team is for each student to be given the opportunity to reach full potential. Teams meet at least once a month and address a variety of issues, but do not deal with any that relate to individual students, teachers, or other personnel, contract agreements, board policy, state laws, rules and regulations. Each person on the team then reports back to the groups they represent. No final decisions are made until everyone has the opportunity for input.

An example of an issue that came up in one district was: How could the school be a safe place despite the increase of violence, crime, kidnappings, and selling of drugs on school campuses? The team brainstormed ideas and decided that all parents and visitors to the school needed to wear stickers that would identify them. People without these stickers would be directed to the office in order to get one. The team felt that, unless students felt safe, it would interfere with their academic achievement. Issues discussed may be different in each school due to meeting the needs of that particular situation.

Programs, such as Shared Decision Making, allow parents to be directly involved in deciding issues that affect their children.

Parent-Teacher Organizations/Parent-Teacher Associations

The PTO and PTA facilitate communication between faculty, staff, and parents. They help bridge the gap by opening the door for parental involvement in the schools. They encourage teachers to want parents in the classroom. In order to do so, they provide nonthreatening activities for parent participation. They instill in parents that confidentiality is extremely important and classroom involvement is not an invitation to gossip outside the classroom door.

The PTO or PTA groups may assist teachers by supplying room volunteers. Some offer money for special projects. They organize student activities, such as roller-skating parties, author visits, carnivals, plus a wide range of other special events. The PTO/PTA can also be a great resource for special activities and curriculum expansion.

Weekly or Monthly Family Nights

Organizing nights on a weekly or monthly basis gives families a place to participate in activities together. The most popular activities include ball games, board games, movies, arts and crafts, roller-skating parties, volleyball, and basketball games. The thought behind this approach is to get parents to come to school for fun activities and to make them feel comfortable in a school setting. It also encourages and models positive parent/child interaction. Those feelings will eventually carry over into the regular school day.

High-School Involvement

Parents with children in high school often find their only way of involvement centers around sports, music, or drama. Not all parents have children who participate in these events. Therefore, it is very important to offer other alternatives. High school teachers who responded to my survey concerning involving parents listed the following examples:

- Participate in or lead book reviews.
- Tutor students.
- Offer technology help, present computer programs, or help students design their own computer program.
- Participate or arrange a career day involving parents from a wide variety of career choices.
- Organize a foreign language night. Prepare international foods, dress in appropriate clothing from other countries, invite a guest speaker to show pictures and speak about a country.
- Lead drama or art programs.

PARP

The PARP, also known as Parents as Reading Partners, is a program that encourages parents and children to read each day at home for an allotted time. The objectives of this program are to develop a positive attitude toward reading and develop lifelong reading habits. The program recognizes that development of a positive attitude toward reading cannot be developed solely in school. The home plays a major role in this achievement. For many years prior to the 1990's, parents read with their children. Nightly bedtime stories were an intimate sharing between child and parent, which helped both reflect on, and unwind from, a hectic day. In the 1990's, with the breakdown of family units, this nightly ritual has been lost in the process. If you do not have a PARP program at your school, turn to Appendix A where you will find information to get you started.

Doughnuts for Dads and Muffins for Moms

The Parent Teacher Association at Jackson-Keller Elementary School in San Antonio, Texas, hosts before school parties—Doughnuts for Dads in the fall and Muffins for Moms in the spring. This allows parents the opportunity to visit school in a relaxed setting. Parents who participate feel more comfortable and at ease in the school setting. Due to busy work schedules, they still are able to be involved in their child's education. The PTA finds this a very successful way to lure busy parents into school to talk, while enjoying a doughnut or muffin.

I plan to implement this program, once each month, in my own room next year. The day before, students will prepare the food. Parents will be invited to bring their child to school, have a cup of coffee and something to eat. On display in the room will be samples of work and projects. Students can "show off" their room and do some "bragging." Also, I will be able to answer any questions and avert any potential problems.

Reaching the New Parents

At Dann C. Byck Elementary School, in Louisville, Kentucky, the parent group gives child-care pamphlets to families of new neighborhood babies. As the babies grow, the parent group lends out age-appropriate books, toys, and games. This appears to be a great program for building a positive image of school.

Community-Parent Education Program

Lori Deptula, a part-time social worker from Tully, provides parents with a parent education program. Among some of the topics addressed are: sharing of child management skills, encouragement of positive behavior, increasing social skills, promoting self-esteem, getting children to do what you want to do, avoiding unnecessary conflicts with children, developing an effective incentive system for children, and creating a plan to improve children's self-control.

The program runs for two hours on a weeknight for a period of eight to ten weeks. More and more schools are offering parenting programs to help parents improve their skills. Many problems encountered in schools today reflect parenting problems. Every job in this country requires some type of training, but the most important job—raising children—offers no training. Educating parents in these skills and problem areas results in better parents, more school support, and a better educational system because teachers can teach without having to deal with disruptions.

Los Angeles Parent Institute for Quality Education (LAPIQE) in collaboration with World Vision offers a nine-week parenting course for low-income minority parents of elementary students. They seek to help parents take an active role in assisting their children to: stay in school, improve classroom performance, improve parent/child relationships, and enhance ability to attend college.

The objective is to build strong parental involvement in the educational process at home and in school. The course is taught in the morning and evening to accommodate working parents, no matter which shift they work. Topics include home, motivation, self-esteem, communication, discipline, home/school collaboration, drugs, college and career electives, and how the school as a whole functions. They have found parental involvement has improved the school environment and increased student achievement.

Parent Bookshelf

Scholastic Book Club offers The Parent Bookshelf to parents through the school. Books are offered to parents to help their children via parenting books, software, videos, and educational toys. Teachers send home a flyer to parents similar to those for student book clubs. Parents who order send the slip and money back to the classroom teacher. For further information contact Scholastic Book Club, Attention: Parent Bookshelf, 2931 East McCarty Street, P.O. Box 7502, Jefferson City, MO 65102-9968.

Parent Resource Room

Malholm Elementary School in Lakewood, Colorado, has a parent resource room complete with washer, dryer, computer, microwave, and sewing machine. The room is open afternoons and evenings for parents and children. A social worker staffs the room to help parents with continuing-education programs, resumes, job-hunting information, and information concerning a General Education Diploma. The goal is to give parents a reason to come to school and meet school personnel who care about families, and still finish "home" chores.

Report Cards for Parents

Every six weeks at Frederick Douglass Elementary School in Dallas, Texas, when students get their report cards, they also take one home in which they have graded their parents. Students grade parents in six "subjects": praising and hugging your child, reading to your child, making sure your child is prepared for school, helping with homework, visiting the school, and attending parent-teacher meetings. Younger students draw happy or sad faces, older ones give letter grades. Former principal Patricia E. Mays wanted to get parents involved in their child's education and give the children a way to communicate their needs and expectations to their parents.

Since the introduction of parental report cards, student and parental attendance at the school has improved. What a great way for busy parents who are constantly pressed for time to realize it only takes a few minutes to hug their child, to help the child get ready for school, and so on.

Child Placement

In the spring, Principal Ruth Groves Ryan sends out a letter to parents asking for input on their children's academic strengths/ needs, social/emotional needs, other pertinent information, and children their child should be kept away from (Figure 3b). This questionnaire enables her and the staff involved in organizing class lists to make sure the very best placement is made. Parents feel better knowing their input is valued and used.

TYPES OF CLASSROOM INVOLVEMENT

It is wise to survey parents at the beginning of the school year to find who is available to help and those who have special talents or hobbies to share (Figure 3c). This will help determine what parents are available to help during school hours and those who could do a mini-lesson on a hobby or talent. I've had parents teach classes on basket weaving, bread making, arts and crafts, CPR, and so on. Parents have a wealth of knowledge to share— use them! If they know far enough in advance, many will try to get time off to help with extra activities.

HOMER CENTRAL SCHOOL DISTRICT
HOMER ELEMENTARY SCHOOL

Spring 1994

Dear Parent/Guardian,

Later this spring the staff will be organizing classes for next year and would like to solicit your input as they work to provide the best learning atmosphere for each child. Your input, as well as a host of other information, is used to determine classes which we expect will meet the wide-ranging abilities and needs of our students. The staff must consider the following:

- maintaining a good ratio of achievement levels, special talents, and needs of students
- relationships that students have with one another and their ability to work well together
- maintaining a healthy balance of boys and girls
- personality and work habits of individual children

Using teacher and parent input, measures of achievement, and indicators of special needs, the school staff will decide on student placement and notify you on the last day of this school year when report cards are sent home. (In the case of kindergarten, you will be notified as soon as possible during the summer.)

If you desire, you may fill out the reverse side of this letter and return it to the school by May 6th. Your impressions and observations about your child will be added to all we know to make the very best placement. PLEASE DO NOT MAKE A REQUEST FOR A SPECIFIC TEACHER. You have our assurance that the placement will be with a teacher for the next year who is well-qualified to meet your child's needs.

If you have any questions, please feel free to call me. Thank you for your cooperation and assistance in this important endeavor.

Sincerely,

Ruth Groves Ryan

Ruth Groves Ryan

Figure 3b *Letter to parent asking for input concerning placement.*

Student's Name _____

Present Teacher _____

1. What academic strengths and/or needs do you feel should be addressed? (example—motivation, organization, task commitment, attention, and/or a subject might be mentioned)

2. What social and/or emotional needs would you like us to consider? (example—learning style, relationships with others)

3. Is there any other information that you would appreciate our taking into consideration?

4. Is there a child that you feel your child should be put into a class with or kept away from? If so, who and why? Are there any relatives in the same grade level as your child?

Parent's Signature _____

Figure 3b (continued) Letter to parent asking for input concerning placement.

```
┌─────────────────────────────────────────────────────────────────┐
│                     Parent Questionnaire                          │
│                                                                   │
│  Please check the appropriate phrase.                             │
│                                                                   │
│  _____  I would like to be a room mom or dad. (If more than one  │
│          person signs up you will share this important duty.)     │
│                                                                   │
│  _____  I would like to help in the classroom and am available   │
│          during these times:                                      │
│                                                                   │
│          specify days and times _____    │
│                                                                   │
│          _____ │
│                                                                   │
│          _____ │
│                                                                   │
│  _____  I am unable to help but would like to be involved in any │
│          special events, if I know far enough in advance and can  │
│          arrange my schedule to accommodate them.                 │
│                                                                   │
│  _____  I am unable to help.                                     │
│                                                                   │
│  Please list any special talents or hobbies you could share with  │
│  the class.                                                        │
│                                                                   │
│  _____│
│                                                                   │
│  _____│
│                                                                   │
│  _____│
│                                                                   │
│                            _____         │
│                                   Parent's Signature               │
└─────────────────────────────────────────────────────────────────┘
```

Figure 3c Parent survey.

Cooking Projects

Students love to cook and cooking projects show them how to make things from scratch. Examples include making simple things, like applesauce or bread, to the complex task of preparing the whole meal. Each year my students plan and prepare a traditional Thanksgiving dinner in the fall. In the spring they do another meal. I let parents know two months in advance, so that, if they wish to help, they can plan their work schedule accordingly. I could never attempt a project such as this without parent help.

Sewing Projects

Many students do not know how to sew, so I do projects, such as sewing a Christmas stocking, making a heart-shaped pillow, or making a quilt to give to a homeless shelter. Parents love to get involved in these activities that require actual teaching and working very closely with children.

Volunteers

Volunteers are a great help with slow or advanced children in the class. Use them as a helping hand to prepare bulletin boards or organize activities. Some teachers go so far as to actually train volunteers who will work with students. Parents are scheduled for a specific time and, if they are unable to come, it is their responsibility to find a replacement. When parents know their commitment is essential and depended on, participation is outstanding.

Winter Picnic

A Winter Picnic is a great way to beat those midwinter blues. Have parents help plan activities, bring in grills, and have an old-fashioned picnic complete with hotdogs and salads. In snowy climates a kickball or baseball game in the snow puts even your gifted athletes on the same level as those who aren't gifted.

Year-End Fling

A Year-End Fling is similar to the winter picnic but done the last week of school. This is a great opportunity to recognize those parents who have lent a helping hand throughout the year.

Science Projects/Science Fairs

Science projects bring out the best in some parents and require student and parent to work together to develop a project.

Multiplication Mania

Michelle Dougan, a third grade teacher, found when teaching multiplication tables, she needed to develop a method that would get students and parents excited about drilling them at home. She sent a letter to parents (Figure 3d) asking that they spend ten minutes a night on multiplication tables, starting with zero. When their child passed a timed test in school on those tables, the parent would then work on the next level. At the end of five weeks, a graduation ceremony was planned for students who had passed tables from zero to five. Students made graduation caps and tassels to wear and received diplomas. Parents and students then went back to the classroom to attend a graduation party. Participation was 99 percent. This idea shows that most parents will work at home with their children if they know what to work on.

Interactive Homework Assignments

Giving assignments that the parents and children can work on together helps increase parent/child communication and interaction at home. By offering specific examples, parents will then be able to come up with ideas of their own. Assignments may include: working on family budget, helping to balance a checkbook, calculating projected monthly food costs, setting up a grocery list, or reading the food advertisements for money-saving tips.

Dear Parents,

As a supplement to our math curriculum, we are beginning a program called "Multiplication Mania." Each week we will concentrate on one group of multiplication tables. This week we are beginning with zero, next week one through five.

You will find enclosed a weekly chart. I ask that you participate by joining your child in initialing (p = parent, s = student) the chart each night, following your ten-minute session of review for that week's multiplication tables. Each Monday the past week's chart should be cut off and returned to me. If your child has mastered a group of tables, they may move on to the next one.

Students who complete the program accurately will be awarded weekly with stickers. A date will be set for you to attend a graduation ceremony, complete with caps, and a party following the ceremony.

Thanks for your participation and caring about your child's future. It does make a difference!

Sincerely,

Multiplication Mania Chart

		Mon.	Tues.	Wed.	Thurs.	Fri.
week 6	p	_____	_____	_____	_____	_____
	s	_____	_____	_____	_____	_____

[Continue the same chart for weeks one through five. Start with week one at the bottom making it easier for parents to rip off and return.]

Figure 3d Multiplication mania letter.

Coat of Arms

Send home a copy of the coat of arms as found in Figure 3e. As a family, either draw or answer the following questions on the sheet:

A. Three words to describe our family

B. Something we like to do as a family

C. A personal motto our family lives by

D. The greatest thing about our family

E. Draw the family

F. If we could have a family wish

When completed have the students bring back their answers to share and display. Families love to be involved in an activity that requires thought and participation of all members.

All-about-Me Book

The first couple weeks of school I have students publish their first book, *All about Me*. We brainstorm what kinds of things to put in the book such as families, interests, hobbies, favorite things, self-portraits, as well as other things. I also have a list of questions I would like answered. Some examples are:

- My full name is . . .   I was born on . . . at . . .
- My favorite place is . . .
- When I grow up, I would really like to . . .
- I would like to be better at . . .
- I work hard to . . .
- My favorite game or toy is . . .
- I like to spend money on . . .
- I am unhappy when . . .
- My favorite cookies/food/color/TV show/subject/sport is . . .
- The perfect age is . . . because . . .
- I am proud of myself when . . .
- When I'm twenty-five, I hope I will be . . .
- If I could have three wishes for my future, I would wish for . . .
- When I'm at home, I like to . . .

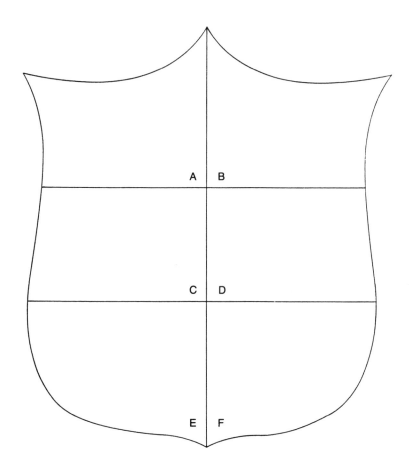

Figure 3e *Coat of arms.*

- My family is special because . . .
- My friends are special because . . .

Have students also ask their parents for ideas that would make their books different from those of their classmates. You will find that parents love to help and the book becomes something they will keep with their child's school memories.

Child of the Week

At the beginning of the school year I write each child's name on a slip of paper and put it in a box. Every Friday I draw a name and that child becomes "Child of the Week" for the upcoming Monday through Friday. I then discard the slip, so that each child is only chosen once.

A note is sent home to the parents (Figure 3f) explaining their obligation, which consists of sending in favorite pictures for dis-

---

Dear Parent,

Your child will be the Child of the Week _____. This is your child's chance to help the rest of the class get to know him on a personal basis.

Your child can send in pictures that will be displayed under the following categories. These will be posted on the back of the room.

My Family
Things I Like to Do
Here I Am
Where I Live
Special Friends
When I Grow Up I Would Like To . . .
My Favorite Toys
My Favorite Food

You are invited to come and read one of your child's favorite picture books. Please let me know in advance the day and a choice of times so I can schedule a time for you.
If you wish, you may send in your child's favorite snack to share with the class.
If you have any questions please don't hesitate to give me a call.
As we make this coming week a special one for your child, thanks for your help.

Sincerely,

Figure 3f *Child-of-the-week letter to parents.*

play on Monday. This helps the class get to know the "Child of the Week" as a unique individual. The parents may choose to bring in a snack and read a picture book, do an activity with the class, attend all or part of a school day, or eat lunch with their child. This guarantees each child one week out of the school year as his week to "shine."

Family Background

When doing a unit on families, have parents and siblings get involved. Make or draw on a map places they have gone on vacation. Put together a class album of favorite family recipes. Have families put together a family tree, family traditions, or a history of the family. You will be surprised at how much history students will learn from one another.

Talent Show

A great way to meet families is to have students plan and produce a one-evening talent show. Students do everything from planning, to final production (including invitations, decorating, serving, and entertaining). Families sign up to bring a dish to share or if you prefer not to have a meal, dessert to share. Each child does a brief performance, such as gymnastics, playing an instrument, mime, puppet show, jazz, line dancing, or singing, for a predetermined amount of time. This is an interesting way to meet families in a relaxing, fun, and nonthreatening way! It is also fun to see each child performing something they like to do.

If you don't have time to do a class play or program that takes a lot of school preparation, this is a great method to use. You only need one or two quick rehearsals to bring it all together.

Adventures of . . .

Send home a stuffed animal, doll, rock, or other item each night with a different student. That night the student and family will write an adventure story concerning the object. You will be amazed at the creativity of some families. Also, creative writing improves due to the constant modeling of story writing.

Parent Homework

Judy Rogers, a second-grade teacher, sends home "Parents' Homework" and invites feedback. The homework is generally an article or newspaper clipping, such as on bolstering the self-esteem of children.

Tea Party

Many teachers have students write, edit, and illustrate their own stories with the end product being an actual book. As a culminating activity invite parents to a tea party where students will be sharing their completed books. Depending on the grade level and length of books parents and students may need to be placed into groups of two to five.

Students love to read to their parents and this is a great way to do so. If parents are unable to attend, visit a senior citizen center, nursing home, or a hospital. If you do not wish to have students "publish" a book then have them write poems or fables. Whatever you choose, the tea party is a fun and relaxing way for students to share their end products.

Working with Inner-City Parents

Carol Sindell provided the following suggestions when working with inner-city parents:

(1) Ask an involved inner-city parent to call other parents.

(2) Get permission from the school bus company to allow parents to ride the bus to school.

(3) Ask parents to share a talent with other parents.

(4) Allow younger siblings to attend with their parents.

(5) Ask for parents' assistance in creating, "Fun Packs" (bags that contain homemade toys, games, and activities). These

packs will circulate around the class for each child to take home for a few days and will allow parent(s) and child to work together.

Miscellaneous

- Plan to weekly invite parents to come in, read a story to the class, plan a game, or do an arts and crafts project.
- Mary Kay Molnar, a primary multiage teacher, states she rarely does anything for herself that a parent could do for her. This frees her of the busy work associated with teaching. She involves working parents by sending home things that might need to be cut out or poems/stories that need to be put on chart paper. She once had a lawyer tell her the most fun he had that day was cutting out the shapes she had sent home that will be used later in a math unit.
- Some community projects that are done in many classrooms include making Christmas, Valentine, or spring cards or small packages for hospitals or nursing homes. Parents' help here makes doing the project go smoother.
- Barbara Mallonee invites parents to come anytime to sit with their child in class. For parents who work at night, this type of involvement allows them to spend time with their child and lets the child know his parent(s) care.
- Plan a culminating activity to end a unit that involves inviting parents to attend. For example, if you are learning about space, teach songs, skits, or poems in which every child can participate. To end the activity, present a final program to the parents. This also reinforces facts about space for the students.
- On any field trips, utilize parents as chaperones.
- Game days go over very well. Invite parents to join in, and there will be fewer arguments among students about cheating!
- Let parents take turns planning and organizing all parties. They love it and it's a big relief for teachers. Some of the best parties in my room were those where parents did everything.
- Joan Osborne uses parents as "ears" to listen to children read. For forty minutes a day she has children read to

parent volunteers. Parents serve as encouragers for new readers, which increases their self-esteem in a newly acquired skill.

- Use parents to help build scenery, design and sew costumes, get together props, work the lighting board, and so on, when doing a class play.
- Carol Sindell provides fun activities for parents like making special gifts for their children at holiday time. Parents have the opportunity to get together and meet others in an informal fun setting.

Tips

- Offer a variety of ways parents can be involved. Even parents who work full-time like to feel they are contributing in some way.
- Be encouraging and supportive. Write personal thank-you notes or use computer or store-bought certificates to thank each parent for any help, no matter how small.
- Treat parents as though they are your equal and that, in different areas, both of you know a lot about their child. You have their child only for a year, whereas they have them for a lifetime.
- Ask parents for ideas or ways to involve them in activities.
- Go beyond the immediate family. Grandparents love to be used, and have enough love and time for all students.

Throughout this chapter you have read a variety of ways that will get parents involved in the classroom. Whatever you choose, remember that most parents are more than ready to help out, but if not asked, will not volunteer. Students love to have their parents visit the classroom and view parents as caring enough about them to participate.

Parents are wonderful resources that are not used as much as they could be year after year. Use them and you will be amazed at the support they offer and knowledge they bring with them.

CHAPTER 4

Documentation

ONE OF THE most important areas many teachers often overlook is the area of documentation. Documentation is something that takes extra time and, with the ever-changing face of education today, it is often the first area that teachers let slide due to other demands.

My first year of teaching I had a student who worked far below grade level and at the first parent-teacher conference I mentioned to the parents I was worried their child may not make it through third grade. Retention was discussed throughout the year, but when it came time in June for the parents to sign a permission slip for their child to be retained, they spoke with the administration and accused me of not telling them. At that point I realized how important documentation was, and have since documented everything pertaining to parents and the children. I hope the ideas presented in this chapter will save you the embarrassment I went through that first year.

Documentation is important when dealing with children who are discipline problems, when you suspect children may need outside help from Chapter One programs to special education placement, or helping you to gain a clearer picture of a student. Documentation allows you to back up what you say with proof. It aids you in presenting a concrete case to parents and administrators when dealing with evaluations, placements, planning, and referrals of students.

Documentation that will be addressed in this chapter deals with anecdotal, classwork, communication with parents in the form of notes and conferences, and discipline problems.

ANECDOTAL

Anecdotal documentation includes information on a student's interests, abilities, behavior, personality, and anything that tells you something about a child. Anecdotal documentation helps you see the chld as a total person based on social, emotional, physical, aesthetic, and cognitive development. Through it you are looking at a broader picture of the total child other than just test scores and daily work.

A great method to keep anecdotal records neat and in one place is to purchase index cards that come in a spiral notebook. Write each student's name on a card and then at the end of the day, week, or month, go through the cards and document any of the following:

- unacceptable behavior
- strengths and weaknesses/what a child can do or not do (usually it is easy to do the weaknesses but with new types of assessment it is extremely important to look for achievements the child is making in the room; look for strengths that may qualify a student for advanced work or programs)
- peer relationships (will also help you to remember at the end of the school year to place students who do not get along in separate classrooms the following year)
- incidences involving school personnel or peers (physical and verbal)
- work habits and patterns (incompleted work, time spent off-task, work that is too hard or easy)

This does not need to be a long, detailed report or written in complete sentences. This method is informal and many teachers use notes or a checklist to record data. Both of these examples have plenty of space for comments. Write just enough to help recall the circumstances or situation. What happened, what was observed, and who was involved are all that is needed. This can be done on a daily basis because too many things can happen weekly or monthly and facts are forgotten.

This takes time, but some teachers have lost their jobs, or have not received tenure, because a parent has backed them against the wall. With no written, concrete data, it is the teacher's word against the child's and the parent's. Your job is worth protecting even if it takes a little more time to document events!

You are probably aware after your first few months of teaching that you cannot possibly please every parent. Each year you will have parents who challenge what you say and how you teach. It hurts when you're doing your very best for a child, and the parents make accusations against you. I have been in tears more than once after parents have left conferences. They allowed their confusion to fester and did not communicate their concerns to me in a timely fashion.

As long as you are doing your best, what more can you do? It is important to not dwell on the negative feedback but on the positive, because you will burn out very quickly in the field of education and look for another type of job. This advice is hard to follow at first, but I have learned that you cannot let one or two parents ruin a year. This is why documentation is so important. You will have written proof confirming what has happened.

Some administrators feel that, in the majority of cases, teachers worry unnecessarily about documentation. The best advice is to trust your professional judgement and instinct, and if you think it is best to document, then do so.

One thing about documentation is that, when you see a pattern developing, you can inform parents with concrete data and examples. If you involve parents before the problem becomes severe, they are more apt to work with you. I noticed when waiting to notify parents some of them become defensive and wonder why they hadn't been notified of the problem right away.

There are instances when children go home and say their teacher did this and that. Instead of speaking with the teacher, the parents immediately go to an administrator or board member. If you make no one aware of circumstances, then you may be putting yourself on the defensive, and sometimes in a hostile situation. By involving parents and/or an administrator right away, you can state the facts in an appropriate manner. Above all, remember you are a professional. Trust your own judgement!

Briefly, documentation is important because:

- You are able to detect any recurring patterns or any situations that may be setting those instances off.
- Documenting provides a total picture allowing you to see overall growth.

- It helps you to record situations just as they happened, and not try to recall from memory something that took place a week or month ago.
- By documenting any problem that occurs in the classroom, no matter how insignificant it may seem, you have a written record for future reference if needed. Sometimes those insignificant problems can become major ones.

DOCUMENTING THROUGH INFORMING PARENTS OF STUDENTS' WORK

Daily Work

My first couple of years teaching I had trouble documenting the children who didn't turn in classwork. I finally devised and perfected the method in Figure 4a. List all the students' names on the left, days of the week on top. Throughout the day record work that is handed in corrected. At the end of the day circle anything not handed in, and read any child's name who must take the work home for homework. Any work not turned in by Friday, jot parents a quick note telling them what assignments were not completed. Keep all completed work in folders with each student's name on them. These are the beginning stages of portfolio assessment.

Pamela Haack, a third-grade teacher in Florida, and an author, uses the above idea but in another way. She runs off a task sheet (see Figure 4b) for each child and hands it out on Monday.

	Mon.	Tues.	Wed.	Thurs.	Fri.
Jessica	S ○ ✔	SS R	M S ✔		
Zach	S M ✔	SS R	M S ✔		
Alex	○ M ✔	SS R	○ S ○		
Shannon	S M ✔	○ R	M S ✔		

Figure 4a Classwork record keeping.

Task Sheet

Name: _____

Behavior Comment: _____

Week: _____

Parent Signature: _____

Subject	Monday	Tuesday	Wednesday	Thursday	Friday

Figure 4b Task sheet.

Throughout the week the child writes the assignment or project due each day. At the end of the day Ms. Haack places a check in the box if the assignment has been completed. If not completed, she circles the box. Once the assignment is completed she then puts a check mark in the box. On Friday the task sheet is sent home attached to all the written work completed in class. A place for a comment concerning behavior is completed by Ms. Haack. Parents look over their child's task sheet and attached work, sign the sheet and return it to school. She keeps all task sheets in her file cabinet for future reference.

No matter which method you choose, the parents will be kept abreast of their child's work habits and actual work on a weekly basis. Parents can also expect that the work from the week will be sent home on Friday and in a very organized manner. Let's face it—most parents work and just don't have the time to sit down during the workweek to look over papers. By giving parents the weekend, they have a more relaxing time to leisurely look over the work from the week.

In both methods above, work is saved in a folder and sent home on Fridays. You will instantly be able to verify when a student who's asked for their work says, "I handed it in." Of course if they did it, it will be in their folders! I have students select two of their best papers. One is displayed on the bulletin board in the room and the other placed in their portfolios. If you hate keeping up with bulletin boards, this is wonderful because the students do all the work. It is also a great self-esteem builder. I sometimes add stickers, my comments, or a blue ribbon on the papers. Ms. Haack has students select two papers that are then put into each student's portfolio.

Progress Reports for Resource Students

Jean Ann Zenker, a resource teacher, sends out progress reports to teachers of her students at the third and eighth week of each marking period (see Figure 4c). She has the teachers fill them out, return them, and then copies them, and mails them to the parents. She puts a copy in each student's folder for documentation purposes.

Homework, Grade Sheet

In some districts weekly progress reports are sent home on stu-

Third- or Eight-Week Progress Reports

Teacher: _____   Class: _____

We need to know how _____ is doing in your room, to date.

1. Are all assignments done up to date?   Yes   No

2. If not, please list the missing ones that you are still willing to accept.

3. List all grades, to date, that you have for this student for this quarter. Or list current average.

4. How is student's attitude/participation and conduct in your room?

5. Did student use his/her testing and classroom modifications as appropriate? (time extension, special location, special notes, calculator, word processor)

6. Does this student appear to need more help?

7. Does student use time wisely in your room?

8. Please comment on the following:
    Attention to task:

    Organizational skills:

    Ability to "keep up:"

    Note taking skills:

    Please return to Mrs. Zenker as soon as possible. These reports will be mailed to parents.

Figure 4c *Resource progress report.*

dents as needed. These include a checklist on test and quiz grades, homework, behavior, and attitude. Although more time consuming, it allows parents to know weekly of any progress or weaknesses. Many times, if a child is failing at five weeks, it may be too late for some to get their grades back to passing. Weekly reports help students and parents know what progress, if any, has been made.

Shirley Howell, a fifth-grade teacher in Louisiana, has devised a homework grade sheet that is used in three states (Figure 4d). The grades accumulate each week until report cards. Under the heading "no homework" or "partial homework" a check is placed in a box if an assignment is not turned in that day.

Signatures on Failed Tests, Projects, Classwork

Many teachers send home failed tests, projects, or classwork for parents to sign and return to school. This method lets the classroom teacher know parents have seen the failing work and are aware of potential problems.

Failing work can be kept in each student's folder allowing the teacher to recognize students who have improved so that the teacher can reward them. It is important to let students know when they are improving and also to notify their parents. Students and parents may see it in a child's grades but to acknowledge the effort makes a big difference. Also, by keeping failing work a teacher can watch for habits or patterns that can be changed.

Five-Week Reports

Five-week reports are a great way to inform parents of their child's progress. Five-week reports are standard in most middle, junior, and senior high schools. Some elementary teachers send out a five-week report but many are not required to. As an elementary teacher, it is important to send out a narrative, five-week failing notice. To avoid writing the same thing over and over, devise a master copy that can be checked off in the subject and problem areas resulting in the failing grade (Figure 4e). This form has saved me a tremendous amount of time and looks much more professional than a handwritten note.

Name _____

Your child's grades as of   /   /95

Reading _____   Math _____

Spelling _____   Social Studies _____

English _____   Science _____

Conduct Grade: _____

Comments:
   Education is as simple as A, B, C; Attitude, Behavior, Cooperation
        + = Excellent   + = Above Average   ✔ = Average
        ✔ − = Trouble's Beginning   − Needs to Improve Quickly

1. Listens and follows directions   _____

2. Is kind to others   _____

3. Keeps desk and work area organized   _____

4. Uses time wisely   _____

5. Walks quietly to and from class   _____

6. Does own work   _____

7. Uses proper restroom/playground behavior   _____

8. Uses proper cafeteria behavior   _____

No homework or partial homework:

Subject	Mon	Tues	Wed	Thurs	Fri
Reading	_____	_____	_____	_____	_____
Math	_____	_____	_____	_____	_____
Spelling	_____	_____	_____	_____	_____
English	_____	_____	_____	_____	_____
Social Studies	_____	_____	_____	_____	_____
Science	_____	_____	_____	_____	_____

Parent Signature _____

Figure 4d Homework grade sheet.

Elementary School Five-Week Notice

Student _____   Date _____

Teacher _____   Grade _____

Your child is failing or borderline in the subjects checked below:

_____ Reading   _____ Math

_____ English   _____ Spelling

_____ Handwriting   _____ Science

_____ Social Studies

Areas contributing to problems:

_____ Poor test scores

_____ Working below grade level; lacking appropriate skills

_____ Work is not being rechecked and/or is sloppy

_____ Poor attitude toward school and work

_____ Assignments are not being handed in

_____ Other:

_____

_____

_____

If you wish to discuss this further, please contact me.

Comments: _____

_____

_____

Figure 4e Five-week notice.

Tully Elementary School Interim Report

Date: _____   Student's Name: _____

_____ 5 weeks   _____ 15 weeks   Grade/Subject: _____

_____ 25 weeks   _____ 35 weeks   Teacher: _____

The purpose of this report is to provide parents with information during the time between issuances of the ten-week report cards. The comments checked below indicate areas of strengths and/or weaknesses.

Preparation and Participation

( ) Is consistently prepared for class

( ) Contributes additional ideas/materials to class

( ) Actively participates in class

( ) Comes to class without appropriate materials/equipment

( ) Needs to participate more in class

( ) Inadequately prepared for tests

( ) Wastes class time

( ) Has difficulty understanding concepts; lacks necessary skills

( ) Frequent absences hamper progress (# to date_____)

Assignments

( ) Completed satisfactorily

( ) Incomplete, poorly done, late

( ) Seldom or never done

( ) Takes advantage of extra credit opportunities

Attitude and Effort

( ) Good, shows interest and enthusiasm

( ) Is attentive

( ) Seeks help when needed

( ) Is self-motivated

( ) Follows directions well

( ) Poor, shows little interest

( ) Is inattentive

( ) Does not seek help when needed

( ) Does work only under pressure

( ) Needs to follow directions more carefully

Figure 4f Interim report.

```
┌─────────────────────────────────────────────────────────────────┐
│                          Behavior                                 │
│                                                                   │
│  ( ) Respectful and considerate of      ( ) Uncooperative and disrespectful │
│      others                                                       │
│                                         ( ) Disruptive            │
│  ( ) Cooperative                                                  │
│                                         ( ) Is too sociable       │
│  ( ) Inconsiderate towards others                                 │
│                                                                   │
│                        Quality of Work                            │
│                                                                   │
│  ( ) Is outstanding                     ( ) Has deteriorated      │
│                                                                   │
│  ( ) Is good                            ( ) Is inconsistent       │
│                                                                   │
│  ( ) Has improved significantly                                   │
│                                                                   │
│  Comments: _____ │
│                                                                   │
│  _____ │
│                                                                   │
│  Teacher's Signature _____  │
│                                                                   │
│    If you feel the need to discuss this report, please call the teacher for an appointment │
│  at 696-6213.                                                     │
├─────────────────────────────────────────────────────────────────┤
│                                                                   │
│  Please sign and return the yellow copy.                          │
│                                                                   │
│  Parent's comments _____   │
│                                                                   │
│  _____ │
│                                                                   │
│                    Parent's Signature _____   │
└─────────────────────────────────────────────────────────────────┘
```

Figure 4f (continued) Interim report.

Cortland Jr./Sr. High School Interim Report

To the Parents of: _____   Teacher: _____

Grade: _____   Date: _____

Subject: _____   Homeroom: _____

Commendation Report
Present mark is _____

The following items indicate the reasons for this commendation:
- ☐ Makes a positive contribution to class
- ☐ Is a regular participant in class discussions
- ☐ Prepares assignments thoroughly and neatly
- ☐ Devotes a great deal of effort to work in the subject
- ☐ Follows directions
- ☐ Prepares well for and does well on tests
- ☐ Works independently
- ☐ Is considerate of others
- ☐ Works to the best of his/her ability
- ☐ Seeks teacher help when needed
- ☐ Is a good role model

Deficiency Report
Present mark is _____

The following items indicate the source of difficulty:
- ☐ Request parent conference
- ☐ Needs to see teacher for extra help
- ☐ Prepare assignments on time; does not meet deadline
- ☐ Attendance has been irregular/owes back work
- ☐ Needs to pay better attention in class
- ☐ Should put more effort in classwork
- ☐ Should devote more time to homework
- ☐ Work is carelessly and poorly done
- ☐ Seems to lack aptitude or interest for subject
- ☐ Comes unprepared to class
- ☐ Does poorly on test/quizzes
- ☐ Needs to improve behavior in class

Teacher comments: _____

_____

Parent comments: _____

_____

Parent/Guardian Signature: _____

Figure 4g *Interim report—Cortland.*

Homer Central High School
Homer, New York 13077
Telephone 749-7241

INTERIM REPORT

Student's Name: _____   Date: _____

Grade: _____   Teacher: _____

Subject: _____   Counselor:_____

NOTICE TO PARENTS

_____ Student is **in danger of failing this course.**

_____ Though currently passing, student is not achieving his potential.

PROBLEM AREAS

Classwork

_____ Attitude in class needs improvement
_____ Behavior in class is unsatisfactory
_____ Doesn't participate in discussion
_____ Absent _____ times from class
_____ Doesn't take adequate notes
_____ Unsatisfactory exam scores
_____ Doesn't make good use of work time in class

Homework

_____ Rarely, if ever done
_____ Sometimes not done
_____ Usually done but incomplete or careless
_____ Is late with assignments
_____ Leaves long term projects until the last minute

Other

_____ Doesn't do reading assignments
_____ Doesn't study to learn concepts, fromulas, dates, etc.
_____ Doesn't come in for extra help as suggested
_____ Isn't making satisfactory progress on projects or labs
_____ Fails to bring books/supplies to class

Figure 4h Interim report—Homer.

Additional teacher comments: _____

_____

_____

_____

Student comments: I have read the comments by my teacher and resolve to do the following to improve my performance.

_____ Improve classroom behavior
_____ Attend class regularly
_____ Come prepared for class
_____ Turn in satisfactory work on time
_____ Study for class and tests
_____ Come in for extra help

Other: _____

_____

_____

_____

Parent comments: _____

_____

_____

_____

Parents are encouraged to make appointments with teacher and/or counselor. After parent has seen this report, it is to be signed and the yellow copy returned promptly to the Guidance Office.

Distribution of Copies: White—Parent; Yellow—Guidance Office; Pink—Guidance Office

Student Signature _____

Parent Signature _____

Figure 4h (continued) *Interim report—Homer.*

Another example of a five-week report is a form that Tully Elementary School revised from the high school. This form is called an interim sheet (Figures 4f, 4g, and 4h). Most teachers in grades four through six use this sheet to inform parents, not only of weaknesses and poor work, but also of strengths.

In most cases parents have been contacted for below average or failing work before the five-week point. The notice becomes just a formality.

Signature on Tests and Quizzes

Barbara Mallonee puts all tests and quizzes from the week together on Fridays and includes a cover note that asks parents to sign the papers and to supervise corrections. Although not 100 percent successful, her parents appreciate the consistency. In this way her parents are aware of all grades, not just the failing ones.

Homework Pad

Judy Rogers has her second graders copy their homework into a pad that their parents sign. To make sure the assignment has been copied down, each student has to hold up his pad when done. She quickly walks around glancing at each pad. This identifies students who do not copy anything down.

This is a great idea for letting parents know what the assignments are so no guesswork is involved. We all have those students who, when home, suddenly "forget" what the assignment was or that they even had homework. With the use of the pad, this problem is eliminated.

When appropriate Judy writes notes on the pad and parents do the same. By communicating with parents in this manner, any questions, concerns, or problems can be dealt with immediately and do not fester over time and become a major worry.

Phone Calls

Each time you call a parent or they call you, write down in the back of your planbook what the nature of the conversation was about. I always have a pad of post-its by the phone so I can jot down information and place the post-it in my planbook. At the end of the year I can easily separate and compile phone calls on each student.

Child Calls Home

Having a child call home or the parent's workplace when in trouble is an effective discipline technique. Most parents do not want to be bothered during the day and in most cases one or two of these phone calls solves the problem. The child tells the parent what he did wrong, the consequences of their actions, and future expectations for behavior. The teacher also speaks briefly to the parent.

This particular method works well because you are present to hear what the child tells the parent. The child hasn't had time to change the story or "soften" it. The truth is being portrayed exactly as the problem happened. When using this method, it is 100 percent effective. Also, when other students in the class know you will actually have them call their parents, they are less likely to push their luck.

DOCUMENTING PARENT CONFERENCES

Conferences allow parents the chance to sit down and discuss their child's work and any questions they may have with the teacher. Conducting successful conferences takes experience, patience, and practice. Conferences can be very stressful and tiring. It is sometimes hard not to take the defensive when parents are unhappy and perhaps accusing.

Make sure when conferencing you write out in advance what you wish to discuss, always stating the child's strengths and areas of concern. Don't think you will remember points you wish to make. If your district gives you a day to conference, you will find that after a few conferences, you begin to wonder what you have and haven't said. Also, by writing down the contents of the conference, you have documentation of what was discussed.

Some teachers like to use index cards at the time of the conference. They include the child's name, parents' names, and comments pertaining to problems, strengths, and weaknesses. I use the form (Figure 4i) to check off and briefly list what I wish to dis-

```
┌─────────────────────────────────────────────────────────────────┐
│                    Tully Elementary School                        │
│                    Parent-Conference Form                         │
│                                                                   │
│  Student _____  Teacher _____   │
│                                                                   │
│  Age _____      School Year _____                       │
│                                                                   │
│  Request for Conference:    Teacher: _____     Parent: _____│
│                                                                   │
│  Other: _____ │
│                                                                   │
│  Background Information            Curriculum                     │
│                                                                   │
│  _____ Family History         _____ Classroom Routine   │
│  _____ School Records         _____ Academics           │
│  _____ Special Circumstances  _____ Special Subjects and │
│                                                 Services           │
│                                    _____ Other               │
│                                                                   │
│  School Policies, Programs or                                     │
│    Services                        Report Card Explanation        │
│                                                                   │
│  Expectations:                                                    │
│  A. _____ Teacher             _____ Marking System      │
│     _____ Parent              _____ Grades on Card      │
│     _____ Student                                            │
│  B. _____ Academic                                           │
│     _____ Behavioral                                         │
│     _____ Preparedness                                       │
│                                                                   │
│  Comments/Recommendations: _____ │
│                                                                   │
│  _____  │
│                                                                   │
│  _____  │
│                                                                   │
│  _____  │
│                                                                   │
│  _____  │
│                                                                   │
│  Has possibility of retention been discussed at this conference?  │
│  _____ Yes      _____ No                                      │
│                                                                   │
│  Next Conference  _____ As needed  _____ Year end  Date: _____│
│                                                                   │
│  Areas checked above have been discussed. Date: _____         │
│                                                                   │
│               Teacher Signature_____  │
│                                                                   │
│               Parent Signature_____  │
└─────────────────────────────────────────────────────────────────┘
```

Figure 4i Parent teacher conference form.

cuss. I sometimes have parents sign the bottom, if I am discussing something that may get sticky (especially retention). In some districts, it is mandatory that both teacher and parent sign the conference report, and that parents retain a copy. Again, this is done to protect you from any potentially unpleasant situations.

In cases where you think a conference may get sticky, invite an administrator or another teacher to sit in. This way you have backup in case a parent later tries to accuse you of saying something you didn't.

Tips on Conducting Successful Parent Conferences

(1) Do not compare or mention other students. Parents are there to talk about their child, not other members of the class. Be professional at all times.

(2) Stick to the topic of reason for the conference. By planning an agenda, you will not forget to mention important items. Be prepared!

(3) Keep on schedule! Most conferences should be no longer than fifteen minutes. Schedule the students who will need more time on another day, or plan an extra time slot. If you have a line of parents waiting, your conferences are running too long. This means you're on a sour note before even beginning. (Think of the times you've waited in a doctor's office!)

(4) Offer phone conferences for parents who cannot make the time slots available. Don't punish parents by refusing to conference because their schedule doesn't permit it.

(5) Display the student's work in waiting area. This allows parents to have something to look at if they arrive early.

(6) When greeting parents always extend your hand, smile and use eye contact.

(7) Don't talk about yourself. This may seem silly, but some parents have told me they have gone to conferences where the teacher discusses his personal life instead of discussing the child.

(8) For parents who bring small children, have toys, color sheets, and books available for them to play with. This frees a parent from keeping a child quiet or holding them.

(9) Don't share so many things with the parents that the most important points become hidden.

(10) Don't be all negative. Start out with something positive, and leave parents with something positive at the end. A good practice to follow is to give two positives before each negative.

(11) Use the phone for conferences to address minor problems.

(12) Don't let parents back you against a wall, therefore causing you to say something you may regret. If you do not know the answer, say so, and tell them you will get back to them later.

(13) Do not talk down to parents. You are working *with* parents to help their child experience success in school. That is your common denominator!

(14) The steps you should follow during the conference include

- Welcome the parent(s).
- Present purpose of conference and information.
- Allow time for parent questions and/or comments.
- Wrap up the meeting.
- Jot down any plans for follow up.
- End on a positive note.

DOCUMENTING COMMUNICATION WITH PARENTS

The third area to document encompasses any communication via notes or phone calls to parents. Any time you send home correspondence to parents, make sure you save a copy for yourself. This is very important, especially if a parent claims never to have received a copy. When sending home important information to a parent, always send it in the mail. Don't rely on a child to deliver something to his parents.

I have found it helpful to keep a folder or large envelope in the front of my file cabinet labeled "parents." This contains all the written communication parents have sent and conversely. If a parent sends in a note, it is stapled to my reply to the parent's letter before putting it in the folder. If a parent wants me to call, the time and date I called and the nature of the conversation are recorded on the note. When I initiate a phone call, it is recorded, with the date, in the back of my planbook, whom I spoke with, and the reason for the call. At the end of the year the important information is put in the child's cumulative folder. However, for safety's sake, I never throw out any information until the following year is over.

DOCUMENTING DISCIPLINE PROBLEMS

Most educators would agree that one of the toughest areas teachers face today is that concerning misbehavior in the school and the classroom. Many states have seen a drastic increase in the rates of violence and discipline problems in the past several years. Discipline problems have become a nightmare from the rural to suburban and city schools. No school is exempt, as both public and private sectors struggle to stop the steady increase of discipline problems.

Everyone knows that in order to run an effective classroom, discipline problems must be kept to a minimum and definitely at a controllable level. Due to the severity of problems facing teachers today, ways must be found to get parents involved and be supportive. Without the backup from parents, many teachers find they are up against a brick wall. Almost every teacher who has spoken to parents concerning discipline problems has had the parent who said, "It's not my problem. It happened in school. You deal with it." The days have disappeared when children who were disciplined for trouble in school would also be disciplined at home. Parents stood behind the teachers and supported them.

As teachers, we have to make parents realize their support in the process and consequences is vital. We need them on our side. The rest of this chapter addresses the documentation of discipline problems and gives some general tips.

The first step in informing parents of the classroom discipline policy is to let them know from day one what behavior is acceptable and not acceptable. Some schools have handbooks created by a team, consisting of parents, students, teachers, and administrators. Among the topics covered are the schoolwide discipline policies. Parents can turn to this to see what behavior is expected and the consequences when that behavior is not met.

Many teachers have found it very beneficial to send home a letter to parents explaining the classroom discipline plan by listing the rules and consequences. In the letter it is important to explain that it is in their child's best interest that, should any discipline problems arise, you will both work together. With their support you will be able to provide an educational climate conducive to learning. By stating this you have made it clear that you expect their help and cooperation.

After the parents have read the letter, discussed it with their child, added any comments they may have, they sign a form similar to Figure 4j and return it to school. This form should be saved and filed in case a problem arises and a parent states they were unaware of the rules.

A word of caution—when setting up rules, make sure you do not list more than five. It is very unrealistic to expect students to remember more than that. Some schools have had parents and teachers work together to list five rules that are used schoolwide. This way it is easier for parents and students to know what is expected because it is the same each year. Clumping rules together under one heading eliminates the need for several rules all meaning the same thing such as: Do not pinch. Do not hit. No kicking. These would fall under the category of, "Keep your hands, feet, and objects to yourself."

Once the school year is under way, it is important to have

My child and I have read the letter concerning the classroom discipline plan that listed the rules and the consequences.

Student's Signature _____

Parent Signature _____

Daytime phone number _____ Mother _____ Father

Comments _____

_____

_____

Date _____

Figure 4j Signature on discipline plan.

Name	Monday card 1 2 3 4 5	Tuesday card 1 2 3 4 5	Wednesday card 1 2 3 4 5	Thursday card 1 2 3 4 5	Friday card 1 2 3 4 5
Jess					
Catie					
Matt					
[A space may also be added for comments.]					

Figure 4k *Record keeping of discipline problems.*

parent support in dealing with discipline problems by keeping them informed when their child's behavior is positive. You can do this through occasional phone calls, or on interim reports every five weeks (see Figures 4f, 4g, and 4h). If parents know you are aware of their child's positive behavior, then, if you need their help, they are more apt to work with you.

When dealing with discipline problems in class, it is extremely important to deal with them in the quickest way possible. Once you interrupt the flow of the lesson, it can sometimes be impossible to get the class back on task. A method that works extremely well is to use library-card envelopes for each student. Put in five cards (each a different color). When students misbehave, they draw the first card, which is a warning. The next card is a timeout. The third time recess is taken away. The fourth time they call their parents, and the fifth time they are sent to the office. At the end of the day you can record on a master sheet what cards are pulled by using a check mark (see Figure 4k). This helps when informing parents of problems.

Sandy Lynch, a third-grade teacher, developed a time-out sheet (Figure 4l) that a student must fill out when he pulls his second card. This way students must think about what they did wrong and how they must change their behavior in the future. She sends the timeout sheet home at the end of the day for parents to sign and return. She places these in a folder for documentation purposes in case she needs them later.

At the junior-high and high-school level, many schools have referral forms teachers must use, such as the example in Figure

Time Out

Name _____   Date _____   Time _____

1. What did I do? Why am I having time out?

_____

_____

2. Why is my behavior wrong? Why shouldn't I have acted or reacted the way I did?

_____

_____

3. Who controls my behavior?

_____

_____

4. What should I have done?

_____

_____

5. This is what I'll do next time . . .

_____

_____

6. Right now I feel . . .

_____

_____

Golden Rule
Gus

Figure 4l Time-out sheet.

4m. The parent, teacher, guidance counselor, and principal each get a completed copy. Teachers write down what happened and check off the appropriate action taken. The form is then submitted to the principal for further action.

One principal uses a file system to keep track of students sent to her office for disciplinary reasons. She writes down the date and reason for the visit on a five by seven index card along with what the consequence was, such as discussion, lose recess, etc. She calls parents if the problem is severe (child has left classroom

---

Cortland Junior-Senior High School
Discipline Referral

Student's Name _____   Date of Event _____

Homeroom # _____   Grade _____

Student Sent to Office _____   Sent to Time-out _____

Event took place in: Period of Day (Circle one)   1 2 3 4 5 6 7 8 9

Or Time of Day: _____ a.m.   p.m.

Classroom # _____   Lunchroom _____   Other_____

Description of What Happened and Action Taken by Staff Member.

Action Taken Prior to Referral:
_____ Held conference with student   _____ Detained student after school
_____ Consulted counselor   _____ Telephone conference held
_____ Referred to Dept. Chairperson   with parent
_____ Sent previous report home   _____ Personal conference held with
_____ Sent to Time-out Room   parent
_____ FYI for Administration   _____ Other: _____

Name of Teacher/Staff Member: _____

Figure 4m *Discipline referral form.*

```
Disposition of the Case (Principal)

_____ 1. Incident logged and student sufficiently warned so that there should
            be no recurrence. Refer immediately if case is not corrected.
_____ 2. Parents contacted and their help solicited. Date _____ Call _____
_____ 3. Detentions Assigned _____
_____ 4. Timeout Room      Date: _____
_____ 5. In-school Suspension _____
_____ 6. Out of School Suspension _____
_____ 7. Saturday Detention _____
_____ 8. Notify Bus Garage of Suspension from Bus. Bus # ____ Dates ____
_____ 9. Other: _____

Letter sent home _____        Signature of Principal _____

                                                              Date _____

cc: Parent, Teacher, Guidance, Principal
```

Figure 4m (continued) *Discipline referral form.*

without permission), the child has been in her office several times within a week or two, or the child has been disciplined several times for the same problem. Other administrators may use anything from the computer to a notebook to store information concerning misbehavior.

Severe Discipline Problems

Some types of discipline problems are more severe. These should be documented and parents should be informed. They are:

- cases where an injury to a staff member or another student occurs
- verbal abuse (swearing or inappropriate use of language)
- child refusing to leave classroom
- drugs[1] (using or selling)
- defiant attitude of "I don't have to do this" or "Make me"
- child leaving classroom or school grounds without permission

[1] When dealing with students bringing guns to school or dealing in drugs, the police need to be contacted. In most schools these two problems carry with them an automatic suspension for up to a year.

- failure to hand in assignments
- skipping classes or poor attendance record
- weapons[1] brought to school
- disruptive behavior that does not allow the teacher to teach
- late to class several times
- sudden change of attitude, withdrawal, drop in grades
- stealing

Tips on Dealing with Discipline Problems

(1) Due to the seriousness of some types of problems, make sure you document each instance in detail, including what happened, who was involved, what was said, how it was handled, and the consequences. It is important to stick to the facts only. Give copies to administrator(s) and parents.

(2) When dealing with discipline problems, always send letters by mail. Don't rely on students to deliver them because they will most likely know what's inside the envelope, and the letter will never make it home.

(3) Mike Doughty, a high-school principal, states that parents should be involved from the very beginning. In doing so you can be sure they will be on the teacher's side the entire time. If you wait to inform parents, very often they will ask why you waited until now to let them know about the problem. Instead of cooperating and helping, parents will become defensive.

(4) When meeting with parents, always make sure the child sits in.

(5) Don't bother parents with every little thing their child does wrong. Otherwise, if something major comes up, parents may not be quite as receptive.

(6) When phoning a parent at work, make sure you ask if it is a problem calling him there. For most parents it is not, but whenever it is, set up a time to contact them at home.

(7) The top two methods concerning informing parents of problems are by sending a letter or calling parents.

(8) Mike Doughty says that it is important for teachers to remain firm, fair, and consistent. If they deviate from this,

they will find they have created more problems for themselves.

(9) Document what you have told the student and what the consequence will be. Have the student sign the copy so that a parent can't come back later and say their child was not aware of the situation.

(10) Mitzi McDowell, a retired teacher, stressed that it is highly important to keep a log when dealing with troubled children. This helped her immensely when parents accused her of what she had done and not done.

I know this chapter on documentation may seem a little strong, but I have been involved in, and heard of, many instances where, if there had been documentation, a major hassle could have been prevented. Most parents you can trust, but there are some who will not want to believe even if you have written proof. With a good documentation system in place, you are protecting yourself and your job. You look more professional when you can back up your statements with definite examples.

CHAPTER 5

Assessment

EDUCATORS THROUGHOUT THE country have in the past few years been looking at the ways learning objectives are defined, how to increase performance tasks that will demonstrate what students can and can't do, and how to set standards for achievement that will realistically show how well students have mastered the skill. As a result, many new types of assessment and evaluation models have come to the forefront. Terms like "nongraded," "portfolios," "multiage," "rubrics," "performance based," "learning objectives," and others offer new ways to assess a student's growth and have become the common "lingo" among educators today.

The thrust of new assessment models today focuses on what a child can do or how he performs rather than just on a test score. They also strive to make students part of the process by helping them to learn the skill of self-assessing their work. These models allow teachers to communicate much more effectively with parents concerning strengths and weaknesses of students. If you think of assessment as the process of collecting samples while evaluation is making judgements, then it will be easier to determine the difference between the two.

The research collected from teachers shows that many are being forced into new assessment techniques without proper training or background. This chapter is to help teachers become comfortable with assessment terminology by looking at various methods and the benefits they provide.

TYPES OF ASSESSMENT

Traditional-Style Report Cards

Until a few years ago, traditional-style report cards were the primary way students were assessed in most countries, with the exceptions of New Zealand, Great Britain, British Columbia, and Australia. Parents received a report card every ten weeks that showed their child's progress and effort by using letters or numbers. A space for brief comments allowed very general feedback. Many problems were found with this style of assessment, such as:

- A student's progress, growth, strengths, and weaknesses were not shown.
- Grades were very subjective. A "B" to one teacher may be a "C" to another.
- Students were dependent on teacher evaluation, not on self-assessment.
- A student would not know what was needed to be done to raise grades.
- Self-esteem was lowered in many cases. Why try if you can't do better than a "C"?
- Students who received 90's or A's were rewarded positively. For others, grading could have a negative effect.
- Grading led to comparisons with siblings, extended family member's children, and friend's children.
- Grades weren't effective motivators for many children.

Nongraded Report Cards

The break from traditional-style report cards that is now happening is difficult for some teachers and parents who see nothing wrong with a method of assessment that has been used since the formation of the educational system. However, nongraded assessment offers a more detailed account of a student's strengths, weaknesses, and growth. Students know what they have to do for mastery.

Throughout the years of teaching, a pattern began emerging from parents wanting to know more about what their child(ren) had mastered and what needed improvement or help. In 1993 I decided to expand the traditional method of assessing students by listing skills that were introduced in each subject area and those where mastery was expected. The result was a report card that proved to be beneficial and very informative. Various samples of nongraded report cards are in Appendix B.

A word of caution–when switching to nongraded report cards, make sure that the parents are informed of the change. Some parents may become very upset concerning the change if no one explains why. You must educate the parents when introducing change. This proposed change needs to be presented in a positive light so that parents will have a very clear picture of what their child can and cannot do. The switch will be much smoother. You have to sell the change because some people operate on the theory: If it isn't broken, don't fix it.

One problem to avoid is to make sure your report cards don't become lengthy. The first copy I did was four pages long because irrelevant and subjective information had been included. After a year of working with it, I was able to become much more concise (Figure 5a).

Another problem to avoid is to make sure that each grade uses the same heading and format. It is very difficult for parents who have more than one child in the elementary school to understand the various types of formats and headings. Some grades may have number headings where "1" means mastery, while others may use "M" for mastery. This type of assessment will be more readily accepted if continuity between grade levels is kept. It helps if a parent sits on the assessment committee. Common language concerning formats and headings was a result of parent suggestion.

One of the big advantages to this assessment method is that parents have adequate information concerning their child, and those parents who like to work on skills at home with their child can do so. Children do not have to compete with peers for grades. Also, when students change grade levels, the next teacher has a clearer picture of what each child's strengths and weaknesses are.

The major disadvantage is that students who are motivated to achieve by getting good marks are not able to see a letter or number grade for their effort. Some teachers feel that as adults we are rewarded for our work through a paycheck. The same

Tully Elementary School
Third Grade Progress Report
19__ to 19__

Name_____ Teacher _____

Marking Key: x Not working on at this time   * Denotes modified work

M	V	P	I	H	U
Mastery	Very Good	Progressing	Improving	Having Difficulty	Unsatisfactory
Learning	Consistently	Shows Steady	Shown Recent	Needs more time	
Completed	Does Well	Growth	Growth	and experience	

Attendance													Scott Foresman Reading Levels	
	Legal						Illegal						What Do I See	Level 6
Days Absent													City Spaces	Level 7
Times Tardy													On Parade	Level 8

READING	1	2	3	4
Grade Average				
Effort				
Word Meaning/Vocabulary				
Word Identification/Phonics				
Comprehension				
Study Skills				

MATHEMATICS	1	2	3	4
Grade Average				
Effort				
Understands Place Value				
Rounds to 10, 100				
Adds up to 4 digits with regrouping				
Adds a column with 3 addends				
Subtracts up to 4 digits with regrouping				
Subtracts 3 digits with zeros				
Understands multiplication/division concept				
Multiplies 1 digit multiplier with regrouping				
Does long division with a 1 digit divisor				
Uses appropriate problem solving strategies				
Understands fractions/decimals				
Can identify coins and count coins accurately				
Can tell time to the minute				
Understands and uses measurement				
Identifies geometric shape				

SPELLING	1	2	3	4
Grade Average				
Effort				
Learns Weekly Spelling Words				
Retains Spelling for Own Writing				
Uses Resources to spell Words				

HANDWRITING	1	2	3	4
Effort				
Forms Letters Correctly (1,2 printing, 3,4 cursive)				
Neatness in Daily Work				
Uses Appropriate Spaces				

LANGUAGE	1	2	3	4
Grade Average				
Effort				
Grammar/Identifies Parts of Speech				
Composition (Writing Process)				
Understands and Uses Mechanics				

SCIENCE	1	2	3	4
Grade Average				
Effort				
Uses Scientific Method				
Understands Concepts				

SOCIAL STUDIES	1	2	3	4
Grade Average				
Effort				
Understands Concepts				

WORK HABITS	1	2	3	4
Works well independently				
Works well with a partner				
Works well with a group				
Completes work on time				
Is organized				
Stays on task				
Listens attentively				
Follows directions				
Volunteers information				
Asks questions when necessary				

SOCIAL SKILLS	1	2	3	4
Follows rules				
Plays well with others				
Respects others				
Accepts responsibility				

Figure 5a.

Comments :

1st Quarter

2nd Quarter

3rd Quarter

4th Quarter

Figure 5a (continued).

theory applies to students. They are rewarded for their work by receiving grades appropriate to the effort they put into school. Most students and parents respond to failing marks and want to see change, but if marks are no longer used, how will a student be rewarded?

A solution to the above problem is to use both methods. Many teachers in kindergarten through second grade find nongraded report cards much easier because students are too young to handle grades. Students who try hard but are having problems may soon "turn off" if given bad grades all the time. However, teachers in upper grades feel that students are old enough to understand and take responsibility for their grades. Without grades how do you get a child's attention? By using both methods, students are rewarded for their effort and work, yet parents receive more information as to what their child can and can't do.

Authentic Assessment

Authentic assessment looks beyond the standardized or multiple-choice tests. Its primary purpose is to improve student performance. It focuses on what a teacher expects students to be able to achieve or understand and what actually is being learned.

Authentic assessment, then, is setting performance standard based tasks around the actual learning experiences, such as solving real-life problems. Examples of authentic assessment include portfolios and rubrics, which are discussed in this chapter, plus essays, projects showing skills and knowledge, demonstrations that involve problem solving, experiments, interactive technology, open-ended test items, and teacher observations.

Characteristics of authentic assessment include producing ideas (not reproducing), demonstrating background knowledge, in-depth understanding, and integration of ideas. The major advantage is that this method demonstrates what students can do based on using the skills and knowledge they have acquired.

Portfolios

For years portfolios have been used in several professional fields. However, within the past few years this term has filtered into the educational system. Portfolios are used to collect authentic evidence of what a child can do and what they know. The goal of portfolios is to ensure that one can see the complete picture of development of each child.

The use of portfolios encourages students to become responsible for their own learning by using self-assessment skills, making decisions, and setting individual goals. It helps teachers gain insight into each student and to communicate more effectively with parents, administrators, and the next year's teacher(s). It also helps improve instruction because tangible evidence is being accumulated concerning what a child can do and cannot do. The "bottom line" is that portfolios are a guide to each student's learning.

Why do we need portfolios? As teachers, assessment helps us to evaluate our teaching style and effectiveness. In the same way students should also be engaged in evaluating their learning, setting goals, and fostering responsibility in themselves.

There are a variety of portfolios. Some may be strictly for academics, such as writing, reading, and/or math, while others may also include projects and pictures. Portfolios may contain one or all of the following:

- teacher samples
- teacher observations[2]
- teacher assessment and evaluation[2]
- other teacher records[2]
- selected student samples showing work in progress, completed work, growth, and best work
- student self-assessment including reflections and comments as to why work was chosen, the importance of it, and what it showed
- standardized tests and other testing[2]
- worksheets
- comments and reflections from parents concerning the contents of the portfolio.

The contents of portfolios may be stored in anything from manila folders to pocket folders, accordion-type folders, scrapbooks, trapper keepers, cardboard pizza boxes, photo albums, or three ring binders as well as on a cassette tape or computer disk. Many teachers like to use large pizza boxes because they are

[2]Denotes those that may be stored in individual student portfolios kept by the teacher.

stackable and, should a child drop the box, the contents are not going to scatter across the floor. They are also a little bit more durable and, when covered with contact paper, look much neater when stacked.

Some helpful hints to keep in mind when doing portfolios are:

- Do not create a portfolio for every subject the first year. A good place to start is a writing portfolio. Doing too much too soon can squelch your enthusiasm.
- Make sure the portfolio doesn't become yours, but one to which students have access at all times.
- Encourage parents to view portfolios on a regular basis. If they are unable to visit the classroom, send portfolios home with a sheet for comments.
- Students must take an active role in the selection of items to be put in the portfolios. Part of self-assessment begins with decisions on what is their "best."
- Regularly have students go through the portfolios, perhaps at the end of each month and get rid of anything they no longer want. Otherwise you will have too much at the end of the school year.
- Have students attach a note concerning why they selected each item to be placed in the portfolio because they may forget the reason later. Also, make sure to date the item. The note may be as simple as: I chose this item to be put in my portfolio because _____. You will be amazed at some of the reasons for including things.
- Make sure that parents are encouraged to enter their thoughts concerning individual pieces of work. A note home explaining the parental input at the beginning of the school year will help parents keep up with their part (see Figure 5b). You may wish to make up a standard form that parents fill in, such as, I think that _____'s work shows _____. I am proud of what _____ has chosen because _____.
- At the end of the year sit down with each student and go through the portfolio. Save a few items to pass on to the next year's teacher. The rest of the portfolio should be sent home where it can be kept among other school memories.

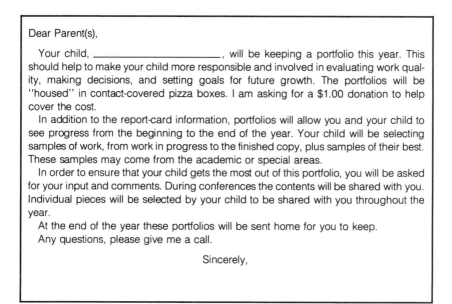

Dear Parent(s),

Your child, _____, will be keeping a portfolio this year. This should help to make your child more responsible and involved in evaluating work quality, making decisions, and setting goals for future growth. The portfolios will be "housed" in contact-covered pizza boxes. I am asking for a $1.00 donation to help cover the cost.

In addition to the report-card information, portfolios will allow you and your child to see progress from the beginning to the end of the year. Your child will be selecting samples of work, from work in progress to the finished copy, plus samples of their best. These samples may come from the academic or special areas.

In order to ensure that your child gets the most out of this portfolio, you will be asked for your input and comments. During conferences the contents will be shared with you. Individual pieces will be selected by your child to be shared with you throughout the year.

At the end of the year these portfolios will be sent home for you to keep.

Any questions, please give me a call.

Sincerely,

Figure 5b Letter explaining portfolios to parents.

- When starting portfolios, it is important that you have listed objectives for each subject. It is almost impossible to assess something if you don't know what you are assessing.

Portfolios are a wonderful way to get parents involved by eliciting their comments on individual pieces. They also give parents the opportunity to see the growth as it is occurring and shows that progress can be measured in ways other than just taking a test. One last word concerning portfolios: Send home a note to parents that describes and defines the purpose of this method as a way of assessment. If parents are going to accept change, they must understand it. Once they do, you will have their full support.

Rubrics

If you took a group of teachers, gave them the same paper to grade, marks would range from "A" to "F." Why? Teachers differ in what they find important. Therefore, if teachers are unclear about what constitutes quality work, then what about students? How can students know what to aim for and measure their assignment accordingly? Very often grades on papers do not tell students what they did well and what they need to work on. All students want A's but very seldom do they know the criteria involved in getting that "A."

As a result, rubrics are now being used in many schools throughout the country. They provide criteria that describe a student's performance via a list of characteristics or checklists. Rubrics help teachers become more focused and precise in what they expect students to know. Figure 5c shows an example that was used for grading a community project. Figure 5d shows how rubrics can help in grading book reports. As you can see from these examples and those found in Appendix C, the subjec-

Grading on Community Project		
	Possible Score	Actual Score
Central Business District	10	_____
Roads	5	_____
Church	5	_____
Houses/Apartments	5	
Attached sheet containing:		
Population	2.5	_____
Name of Community	2.5	_____
State	2.5	_____
Zip Code	2.5	_____
Mayor's Name	2	_____
Natural Resources	9	_____
Places of Interest	9	_____
Neatness	10	_____
Creativity	10	_____
Community is Realistic— contains the following:	25	_____

Rural—farms, animals, lake or pond, general store, trees or forest, hills, grass . . .
Suburban—lots of houses, yards, apartments, drug store, grocery store, streets, park, school . . .
City—lots of buildings where people work, shop, places to have fun, banks . . .

Figure 5c Rubric community grading sheet.

Name _____

BOOK REPORTS

Please select one of the following for your book report. You must select a different one each time. Keep this paper for future book reports.

1. Design a poster advertising the most interesting part of the book. Include the following things:
   title—10 points
   author—10 points
   price if known—bonus 5 points
   color picture of the most interesting part—35 points
   short paragraph (indent, proper punctuation, five sentences, capitals used when necessary)—35 points
   neatness—5 points
   name on poster—5 points
2. Make a mobile with the characters, scenes.
   includes seven characters or scenes—13 points each
   neatness—4.5 points
   name on mobile—4.5 points
3. Plan a TV commercial selling the book.
   name of book mentioned—15 points
   author mentioned—15 points
   expressed to audience why they should buy book—30 points
   mentioned who would like book—10 points
   mentioned enough about book to arouse curiosity—20 points
   creativity—10 points
4. Make a wordfind using characters, setting, etc.
   used fifteen words—4 points each
   list is neat—5 points
   wordfind letters are easy to read and in straight line—20 points
   name on paper—5 points
   name of book and author—10 points
5. Make a puppet of one of the characters.
   creativity—90 points
   name of book shown—10 points
6. List five ways you could have improved the story to make it better—15 points each
   told name of book and author—10 points each
   name on paper—5 points

Figure 5d *Rubric book report grading sheet.*

7. Describe five boring sections—5 points each
   included title and author—10 points each
   name on paper—5 points each
8. Build "shoe box" setting of the story—50 points
   name on project—5 points
   author and title of book displayed—10 points each
   creativity—25 points
9. Design a book jacket (on the inside flap write a short summary of the story)—
   50 points
   outside of jacket must have title—8 points
   author—8 points
   illustrator—8 points
   picture in color—21 points
   name on project—5 points

Figure 5d (continued) Rubric book report grading sheet.

tiveness is taken out of grading. The major advantage is that work is scored accurately and fairly, and no judgement is being made. Students know what is required to get the grade they want.

Rubrics serve many purposes. They let students and parents know strengths and areas needing improvement. Teacher expectations are well-defined in advance. Students know what to aim for, which helps them to meet the requirements for quality work. It also teaches self-assessment skills, focused instruction, and is a reference tool for all. Rubrics give concrete information and, should a parent question a child's score, you have no trouble explaining the score. Rubrics are great for documentation.

When developing rubrics, teachers must draw upon previous students' work as to what is expected, what is typical, unacceptable, and what is needed to demonstrate that learning has taken place. Rubrics are time-consuming to make and take time to revise to fit the standards. A word of caution—if you find that students are all receiving high grades, but performance is not what it should be, the criteria are wrong and the rubric needs to be revised.

Although time-consuming, rubrics are very effective and increasingly popular in the field of assessment. Students are able to turn in higher quality reports, projects, experiments, and papers, because they know exactly what is required. Seeing that students perform at optimal levels is what education is all about.

Learning Objectives

One of the hardest things for a teacher who changes grade levels or for a new teacher is to figure out what is actually a required skill. Many states are now mandating that schools adopt learning objectives that consist of a list of skills that students should master in each academic area by the end of a school year. At the beginning of the school year, some districts hand out a copy to parents of the required objectives for the appropriate grade level. Parents know exactly what is required of their child by the end of the school year. Third-grade learning objectives for math, language arts, and reading may look like the example shown in Figure 5e.

Using learning outcomes is one of the assessment tools that allows teachers and parents to see what is expected by the end of the school year. It also helps teachers stay focused on the curriculum by knowing what needs to be taught.

Continuous Progress

Under continuous progress, students progress at their own rates. There are no retentions, promotions, or letter grades given. Student performance is not linked to the child's age or how long it takes to get through school.

Multiage

Multiage or family groupings is the modern version of the one-room schoolhouse of yesterday that consists of students with various ages and abilities working and learning together. It makes use of the similarities and differences among children and is not based entirely on age alone, as in traditional classrooms. Students are grouped according to abilities, skills, gender, learning styles, and interests. It is not uncommon to see younger children working on advanced skills with older peers and conversely. Placement tests determine beginning points for each child and from there groupings are made.

Multiage is most effective when set up as a team-teaching approach that combines grade levels where students have the same teachers and classmates for more than one year. Students are arranged in "teams" such as K–2, 3–4, 5–6, or K–1, 2–3, 4–6

```
LANGUAGE ARTS

    Student will be able to:
Identify speech parts and show evidence of proper usage of
— singular, plural, possessive, and proper nouns
— past, present, future, regular, and irregular verbs
— pronouns
— adjectives
— adverbs

Use appropriate sentence structure by
— identifying subject/predicate parts
— showing correct capitalization, punctuation of simple declarative and interrogative
  sentences

Demonstrate correct punctuation by using
— period for abbreviation
— comma to separate series
— comma in dates, addresses
— quotation marks to indicate spoken parts in writing

Use organizational and research skills to
— divide words into syllables
— alphabetize to the third letter
— identify entry and guide words in dictionary and encyclopedia
— begin to show evidence of research abilities using a variety of resources including
  dictionary, encyclopedia, texts, books, almanac, phone book, and computer
— follow four-part written directions
— identify and use index, table of contents

Demonstrate writing strategies to
— use a variety of techniques to research, organize and make a rough draft
— produce narrative that is sequentially ordered
— show evidence of beginning editing process
— compose book reports
— produce a persuasive (opinion) essay
— use correct structure in writing a friendly letter

Use handwriting techniques to
— begin writing cursive letters using correct formation

Demonstrate spelling ability by
— showing continued growth in using acquired spelling skills in daily writing
— identifying and sounding out long, short, and irregular vowels
```

Figure 5e Third grade learning objectives.

MATHEMATICS

Use mathematical concepts in:

Addition and Subtraction to
— add/subtract up to four digits without regrouping
— add/subtract up to four digits with regrouping
— subtract three digit numbers with zeros
— add a column with regrouping to four digits with three addends

Multiplication and Division to
— demonstrate concepts by using manipulatives
— identify fact families
— show mastery of facts 0–5
— multiply one-digit multiplier with regrouping
— divide using long division with one-digit divisor and remainders

Problem Solving to
— read, analyze, record data from graphs, charts, and maps
— develop estimating strategies
— analyze and solve word problems using the four processes

Money/Time/Measurement to
— read/write time to the minute
— determine elapsed time
— measure in standard and metric units in weight, distance, volume, and temperature
— solve a word problem by reading a map, calendar, or timetable
— use maps and calendars
— read/write money values through one dollar

Decimals to
— demonstrate meaning of a decimal
— understand and identify tenths and hundredths in a decimal

Fractions to
— identify and write equivalent fractional parts of a region (halves, thirds, and fourths)
— compares fractions

Geometry to
— identify three-dimensional objects
— identify a figure with a line of symmetry
— solve a problem involving perimeter, area, and volume
— identify a pair of congruent figures
— identify right angle, line segments and endpoints
— identify faces, edges, and corners, curved and flat surfaces

Numbers to
— sequence/read/write numbers through 999,999
— identify expanded and standard form for any number to 1,000
— count by 2's, 5's, 10's to 1,000
— identify place value for numbers to 10,000
— compare numbers using greater than, less than or equal
— identify order from least to greatest
— round to nearest 10, 100, 1,000
— identify ordinal position through fifty

Figure 5e (continued) *Third grade learning objectives.*

```
┌─────────────────────────────────────────────────────────────────┐
│                           READING                                 │
│                                                                   │
│   Uses reading skills in:                                         │
│ Word identification to identify and state meaning for             │
│ — prefixes, suffixes, multiple affixes                            │
│ — context/consonants                                              │
│ — synonyms/homophones/antonyms                                    │
│ — contractions/compound words                                     │
│ Comprehension to                                                  │
│ — state main idea                                                 │
│ — make comparisons                                                │
│ — draw conclusions                                                │
│ — identify fact/opinion                                           │
│ — state details                                                   │
│ — identify similarities between words to determine analogies      │
│ — determine fiction/nonfiction selections                         │
│ — state subject of word referent                                  │
│ — predict outcomes                                                │
│ — state author's purpose                                          │
│ — identify sequence of events                                     │
│ — relate cause and effect                                         │
│ Literary interpretation to                                        │
│ — state character/setting of literary piece                       │
│ — identify goal/outcome                                           │
│ — recognize similes and metaphors                                 │
│ — identify forms of literature (poetry, prose, plays, novels, short stories) │
└─────────────────────────────────────────────────────────────────┘
```

Figure 5e (continued) *Third grade learning objectives.*

groupings. These teams create a cluster. Each part of the cluster is in close proximity to the others.

Multiage provides developmentally appropriate education for children, taking them from where they are to where they need to be. By allowing greater flexibility in how teachers teach, instruction can be molded to the way children really learn. Students proceed at their own rates and in their own ways. There is no fear of failure so children can take as much time as needed to master skills or advance quickly as mastery is made.

Students must take the initiative in learning because the teacher is not available every moment. Cooperation among classmates is a vital part of the program. The teacher becomes the classroom facilitator through coaching, modeling, mentoring, observing, and monitoring.

The term, "family grouping," means that families are kept together in one cluster making parental involvement much easier. An advantage for parents is that they become real partners in the educational process and are not only kept informed but know what their role is. When problems arise, parents sit down with the team to discuss the best ways to solve them.

At the end of specific themes, very often there is a celebration for parents, students, and teachers. A cluster may be studying space (each at its own level) and the culminating activity might be a "blast-off" program for parents. Involvement of parents is a key theme.

Proponents of multiage state one of the major advantages of this method is that it emphasizes the process of learning and the development of the "whole" child taking into account how they learn and develop. It incorporates active student involvement consisting of hands-on, concrete experiences based on real-life examples. Multiage provides continuous learning and performance-based testing, which replaces test scores and report cards.

Students are responsible for their own learning. By learning at their own pace, students are encouraged to be self-motivated, self-directed learners who will hopefully enhance their self-concept.

Another advantage is that by having the same teacher each year, the teacher already knows the child and can plan appropriate learning experiences for the following year. Many teachers feel very frustrated in a traditional setting because it seems like they just get to know their students and then it is the end of the year.

Cooperative Learning

Cooperative learning is a method where children of different ages and abilities are grouped together in order to solve problems and/or understand facts or concepts. Each student in the group becomes responsible for the learning and achievement of the others. Upon completion of an activity, each group member must be able to demonstrate mastery. Students are taught to view peers as a source of help in learning. If we are to encourage stronger, positive social attitudes that realistically reflect what is found in the workplace, we need to allow more chances for students to work together in pursuing common goals and developing decision-making skills.

Cooperative learning results in higher-level thinking skills and teaches respect, caring, helpfulness, and cooperation among group members. Through interaction, students get to know one another and appreciate each other's opinions, differences and talents. These factors are not found in traditional settings, where a competitive format is usually taught.

Each member of the group assumes a role, such as facilitator/coordinator, recorder, timer, encourager, and reader. The advantage to cooperative learning is that communication and interpersonal skills are being taught and responsibility for learning is up to the individual. Some teachers even send home cooperative-learning activities for families to do.

This chapter has provided a brief overview of some of the more popular assessment and evaluation models available today. Many changes have occurred over the last ten years as educators try to find ways to improve schools to better meet the needs of students and prepare them for the twenty-first century. In the improvement and creation of new assessment models, students, as well as parents, are being asked to play a more direct role not only in the process but in the outcome. As a result, parents are more informed about expectations, outcomes, and their child's performance. Remember, as you begin to formulate change, start slowly to make the successful transition to newer methods.

CHAPTER 6

Problems Most Frequently Encountered

AS YOU HAVE probably noticed, this book has been very upbeat and positive about informing and involving parents. However, teachers know that not every parent will react positively and questions will arise concerning what to do. This chapter will address these questions and offer some possible solutions.

SOME COMMON QUESTIONS

(*1*) How do I deal with an angry, irate parent?

First of all, let the parent vent, maintain eye contact, and, most importantly, listen without reacting. By listening you may learn if either the parent or you are missing some information pertaining to the problem or situation. Do not interrupt or become defensive. When allowing parents the chance to vent, they are able to let it all out. After ten to fifteen minutes you should state your response. Don't fight parents who are irrational. Staying calm, listening, and avoiding put-downs helps defuse hostile confrontations. Realize sometimes neither side will be able to agree.

(*2*) How do I let parents know when conferences are over?

Generally, if you look at your watch, shuffle the papers, flip the conference form over, and get the next one ready, parents will get the message. If they don't, stand up and suggest another conference or make plans to call them at home.

(*3*) What can I do when parents do not show up for a scheduled conference and do not let me know in advance?

This is a problem for many teachers. Inform parents, when setting dates, to call you at home or during school to let you know if they must cancel. Send reminder notices a few days in advance (see Figure 6a) to jog a parent's memory. Let parents know how important it is that you not to sit and wait for nothing. Sometimes parents need to know a teacher's time is also very important.

Dear Parent(s),

This is a reminder that you and your child, _____ , have signed up for a conference on _____ at _____ A.M./P.M. If, for some reason, this appointment cannot be kept, please call me immediately so that another time can be set up.

Please complete this form and bring it with you to the conference. I will have completed one similar to it. Being prepared in advance concerning what we wish to discuss allows the conference to be more focused and keeps us on task.

Areas of concern:

_____

_____

_____

Other things you wish to discuss:

_____

_____

_____

Strengths you see your child having:

_____

_____

_____

Teacher's Signature _____

Figure 6a Parent/student/teacher conference form.

(4) What difference does it make whether I involve parents or not?

Children who have concerned, involved parents try harder in school because of parental support and enthusiasm for their children. The major difference in the level of school success for most achievers and nonachievers is parent/teacher communication.

(5) I teach inner-city students and send notes home asking for parents to volunteer in the classroom, but no one ever offers. What can I do?

When parents don't respond, a personal phone call that encourages them to volunteer often gets results. Don't assume parents don't want to get involved, or will not help, until you've given it your "best shot." They might need transportation or a babysitter. Try extending personal invitations that will make parents want to be active participants.

(6) Why can't I get parents to support my discipline plan?

Do parents know what your discipline policy is? Many times parents don't know what the rules and the consequences are. In order to support a teacher, parents need a clear picture of what is expected and what is not. Another solution is to have parents and students sign a discipline contract at the beginning of the year.

(7) How do I stop complaints concerning grading?

Make sure you have explained your criteria for grading. Save examples of each student's work. This is why it is important to have parents sign failed tests and classwork and return them to school. By doing so parents have been made aware of the situation. Save the returned work in a folder for future reference.

(8) I invite parents to stop by whenever they want, but no one has ever taken me up on it. What can I do?

Most parents are afraid of interrupting something. Be explicit in your invitation. Let them know the day-to-day schedule. Invite parents to join the class for breakfast or lunch, a special assembly, a class project, for reading, or other specific happenings.

(9) What do I tell a parent when their child is not working up to ability and I can offer no suggestions?

Almost every teacher has had this problem at one time or another. You feel helpless or inadequate. Teachers agree that you should be honest with parents and tell them you don't know how to deal with the situation. This allows you to sit down and brainstorm with the parents and hopefully come up with a workable solution to the problem. Parents respect teachers who admit they don't have solutions for everything. Another suggestion is to contact the school psychologist or social worker to meet with you and the parents to help in brainstorming. Check with other teachers to see if there are other resource persons available in your district.

(*10*) What can I do about a parent who constantly complains about everything?

Unfortunately, in some cases you will encounter a parent who will not appreciate anything you do. You can bend over backwards and it still won't be good enough. In fact, you will find that, no matter what you do, it will never meet their expectations or standards. Ask previous teachers how they worked with the parent. Your best bet is just to cope and survive. Remember to document all communication. Some people are just chronic complainers.

(*11*) How should I handle negative letters from parents?

In cases like this, give the letter and your reply to an administrator to look over. By doing so the administrator is aware a problem exists and has read the reply. If they are contacted by the parent, they already know what has taken place and are more prepared to deal with the situation. Also, wait a day to reread your response to make sure you have written a professional note and not let your feelings intercede. It is human nature to be defensive and angry, but it can't be the undertone of the note or nothing will be resolved.

(*12*) I am so busy at the end of the year, I don't have time that last week to conference with parents concerning standardized test scores. Any suggestions?

Many districts get test results the last week of school making it next to impossible to conference with all parents. Some teachers send home notes informing parents of scores. I personally do this with the latest scores, and also include the previous year's so parents can see the growth that occurred (see Figure 6b). In some districts test scores are only made available to parents who ask for them. If it is too late or too chaotic to have parents come in, but the parents want to know the scores, try phoning and discussing the scores with the parents in the evening.

(*13*) How can I stop parents from appearing at my doorstep every day after school to discuss how their child did that day?

Ask an administrator for help and verify if the parent has checked in at the main office, provided such a procedure exists. If they have, then tell the parent you appreciate their concern but you will notify them if any problems should arise. Sometimes parents do not realize that teachers have meetings, appointments, and other obligations after school. Then excuse yourself to go to one of "your obligations."

(*14*) How can I deal with those children who go home and report what "they thought" I said, and the parents are livid?

Arrange a conference immediately with the parents, child, and administrator. In most cases, by the end of the meeting parents become aware that their child misunderstood what was said and the problem is resolved. It is amazing how the story becomes changed when the teacher is present. Always have the child involved in situations like this because they are the ones who misunderstood what was said.

(*15*) How do I handle situations where I don't agree with the parents concerning their child?

The most important point to remember here is that the parents know their child better than you do. A year in your classroom does not guarantee you know what is best for each child. When you are challenged, back off because parents are in most cases the most important force in their child's education and life.

(*16*) How do I deal with unstable parents who bring their own problems into the classroom when class is in session? I've had parents begin shouting and demand immediate attention. What can I do?

It is unfortunate we live in a time where parents are distraught enough to barge into schools when class is in session. The first thing a teacher must do in cases like this are

Dear Parent,

Below are _____ results for the CTBS tests given in May. A score of 4.9 means fourth grade, ninth month. Grade level results of under 4.0 means that a student will enter fourth grade below grade level in that area. This does not mean your child will not succeed in fourth grade, but it does mean your child had difficulty with these tests.

	Grade 3	Grade 2
Total Battery	_____	_____
Total Reading	_____	_____
Vocabulary	_____	_____
Comprehension	_____	_____
Total Language	_____	_____
Mechanics	_____	_____
Expression	_____	_____
Spelling	_____	_____
Total Math	_____	_____
Computation	_____	_____
Concept and Application	_____	_____
Science	_____	_____
Social Studies	_____	_____

Comments: _____

_____

_____

_____

Figure 6b *Informing parents of year-end standardized test results.*

to assure the child that your feelings toward them have not changed. Children need to know they will not be held accountable for their parent's actions.

If this is a common occurrence, contact your administrator immediately so action may be taken against the parent. In no way is this type of behavior acceptable. Some teachers appoint a child to go for help, if a problem should arise. Other teachers will send the entire class to another room. The teacher can then deal with the parent and not upset the class further. This is serious! Do not try to solve this problem on your own!

(17) A child needs to be labeled and the parents are uncooperative. What can I do?

Sometimes parents will give permission for their child to be tested but not fully comprehend what it means if the child needs to be labeled. Parents need to understand why labeling will be beneficial and the reason why a label is necessary. Information concerning the results of testing needs to be explained to parents in a manner they can understand. Also, make sure they are aware of the difficulty the child might be having in the classroom by giving them the opportunity to observe their child in the classroom setting. Often times this will change parents' opinions.

(18) How can I keep parents informed of monthly behavior of their child? I use the chart in Figure 6c to inform parents. If a child does not pull a behavior card I give them a smiley face for that day. If they pull two cards I write down the last card drawn. At the end of the month I reward students who pulled less than four cards with a choice from the prize box (contains books, puzzles, pencils, posters, etc.). I make a copy of the chart and send the original home to parents. This way parents are aware if their child is consistently pulling cards, but not a severe enough offense that I am calling home. I see a big change in behavior after these charts go home.

Unfortunately, not all problems have easy solutions. The following examples are areas that teachers feel the least comfortable dealing with:

- when a child refuses to do work and you're informed it is your fault

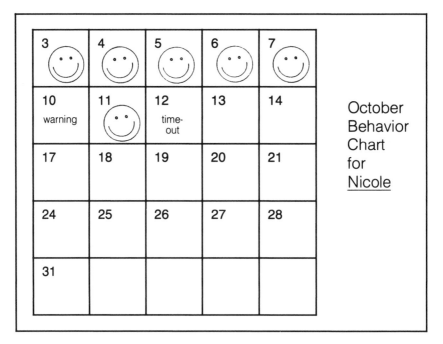

Figure 6c *Monthly behavior chart.*

- parents who take the approach that teachers have failed their child, when the child does poorly on tests and grades in general
- discussing behavior of students, when it is clearly a product of the environment and poor parenting. Unreasonable consequences are useless, because you cannot tell parents how to raise children.
- social problems, such as divorce
- child's weaknesses
- stealing issues
- parents who have trouble taking ownership of their child's disruptive behavior. They make excuses for their child and eventually the child learns how to make his own excuses.
- parents who assume their child is an honor student but has a C average
- dealing with parents whose child needs to be suspended.

It's difficult to break this to parents of children who are "perfect."

- letting parents know that their child is not a "perfect" child, and having parents defend the child, which will not change the child's behavior or attitude
- dealing with parents who are justifiably angry because the child has not reached full potential. It is blamed on the teacher or the systems.
- suspected abuse cases or situations where a child's safety is compromised

These examples show that teachers would benefit from additional help from administrators or from some type of training in handling areas they are uncomfortable with. Many of these areas have to deal with inadequate parenting skills in the home. Parents who work long hours just to be able to put food on the table and keep up with the bills are often stressed to the maximum.

When problems occur beyond the parent's ability to cope, some parents will lash out and blame anyone or anything they can. Often it is the teacher who is the recipient. We've all had the parent, when called regarding a problem, say, "I'm busy. You handle it." Teaching is a difficult field and veteran teachers agree that it has gotten more so in the last few years. Teachers are dealing with more and more problems. There are no easy solutions or quick answers, but just to know that you are not alone helps!

CHAPTER 7

Tips

IN THIS LAST chapter there are many wonderful tips shared by teachers of all grade levels and backgrounds. Some teachers shared their names while others chose not to. I'm sure, when you're done reading these tips, you will agree they are worth remembering!

GENERAL TIPS

Communication

- Suzanne Geer states that from day one a teacher should lay down the rules. Should problems, questions, or concerns arise, parents and students must know the appropriate way to contact a teacher. By knowing what communication channels to use, parents are given the chance to solve problems before they become major.
- Bettemae Russell, a kindergarten teacher, calls *all* of the parents of her students the weekend after the first week of school. This lets parents know how well their child has adjusted to the new school year. This technique allows parents the chance to ask questions and helps set a positive tone for future communication. It also starts the year off positively. Teachers, like Bettemae, who give that extra time and energy, agree it is well worth the investment.
- When handing out your phone number, always give a window of calling time. An answering machine comes in handy when you are busy and do not wish to be disturbed.

- Mitzi McDowell states that conferencing and sending letters home, with phone calls in between, are the best techniques to keep parents informed about their child. Teachers who don't inform parents open the door to trouble in the future.
- Don't talk down to parents. Speak so parents can understand. It is not necessary to impress them with a large vocabulary.
- Send home all information from school once a week. Many parents state they never receive information concerning school events, meetings, or other important information. If parents know information is coming home on a certain day, they will be watching for it. Parents will contact you if they don't receive information when it is supposed to be sent. Put all information in a manila envelope marked on the outside: "To the parents of _____." Write in the child's name and not the parent's due to students not having the same last name as their parents.
- Always make the first phone call or letter a positive one.
- Send the work home on Friday so parents have the opportunity to look at it at their leisure over the weekend.
- Be sensitive to divorced parents. Ask parents if they wish to receive their own copies of report cards, progress reports, and/or newsletters.
- Offer conference times in the early morning, late afternoon, or early evening for parents who cannot take time during their workday. If you don't wish to do this, then offer telephone conferences.
- Set a certain time parents may reach you at home or during school hours.
- Whenever contacting parents, always mention the child's strengths and qualities.

Involving

- Carol Sindell suggests giving parents the opportunity to share ideas and concerns with one another. Parents love teaching, learning, and communicating with one another.
- Include parents in the decision-making process regarding discipline or academic problems.

General

- Barbara Mallonee, veteran teacher, says it is important to keep in touch and remain an ally. She states that we are part of a triangle, parent-teacher-child. When one side fails, the triangle falls apart.
- Treat parents with respect and kindness, and teachers can be expected to be treated the same.
- Try to keep lesson plans a couple of weeks ahead. When parents want work for students who will be missing school, you can accommodate them, or offer homework assignments that fit the vacation (i.e., mileage, distances between cities, number of gallons of gas used, journal of daily happenings, weather, people observed, or to list words found on billboards).
- Send cards to parents who are sick, in the hospital, giving birth, or had a death in the family.
- G. D. Ewald states when working with parents, never compare one child's abilities or disabilities to that of another! Great advice, since we teach that each child is unique.

When dealing with parents, be confident in your professional ability and in discussing your areas of expertise. You are the one who has been assigned to work with this child. Draw upon this strength. As a result of your training, approach a conference or problem with some solution already in mind, but be open-minded and ready to work with the parent. The majority of parents want suggestions from you, whether you are a parent or not. Dealing with problems can most times be solved by working together.

The goal throughout this book was to encourage you to communicate more effectively with parents by offering actual suggestions and techniques. It is hoped that you are more excited about working with parents and including them in your classroom happenings.

If you have read this book and have never tried to establish parent/teacher communications, then you may be feeling rather overwhelmed. Remember, you don't have to do everything the first year. Pick out the things that spark your interest and begin to incorporate them. Once you get going, you will want to do more, and may create your own activities.

In closing I would like to say that I find teaching the most rewarding, challenging, and stimulating job around. There are so many milestones and daily successes that a teacher can share with parents. After all, it is their child we are talking about. You can develop many wonderful memories that involve sharing and utilizing parents in classroom activities. One of the perks about teaching is not only working with children but with parents.

Many very special and lasting friendships can be developed with parents. These friendships have positive implications beyond the personal nature. They strengthen support for the school, help build the school community, and can benefit the entire family, including siblings who later may attend the school. Parents who are excited about school are eager to stay involved and share the positive qualities about school. In a time when federal and state educational budget cuts are occurring and individual schools must make up the difference, it helps to have parent support.

The poem below sums up what this whole book is about. Good luck as you embark on a wonderful journey that will change the way you look at working with parents. When each side of the triangle works together, our educational system will be at its best.

Unity

I dreamed I stood in a studio
   and watch two sculptors there.
The clay they used was a young child's mind
   and they fashioned it with care.

One was a teacher, the tools used
   were books and music and art.
One a parent with a guiding hand,
   and a gentle, loving heart.

Day after day the teacher toiled,
   with a touch that was deft and sure.
While the parent labored by the teacher's side
   and polished and smoothed it all.

And when at last their task was done,
   they were proud of what they had wrought.
For the things they had molded into the child
   could neither be sold nor bought.

And each agreed they would have failed,
   if they had worked alone.
For behind the parent, stood the school
   and behind the teacher, the home.

                Author Unknown

Setting up a P.A.R.P. Program

As you read in Chapter 3, P.A.R.P. is a well-known program that encourages parents and children to read daily at home for an allotted amount of time. In this Appendix, you will find what is needed to set up a program within your school.

GOOD NEWS! IT'S PARP TIME AGAIN!!

Dear Parent(s):

If there is one key ingredient in a student's ability to succeed in school, it is attitude. A student with average or below average ability who works faithfully at a task can often achieve greater success than the student of superior ability who refuses to use that potential.

Development of a positive attitude in a student is something that cannot be developed solely in school. The home plays the major role in the development of the child's attitude and that is the basis for the Parents as Reading Partners' program. How the child perceives a task, such as reading, how he or she feels about it, will determine the degree of involvement and of learning which results.

On November 2nd, Tully Elementary School will launch a "Parents as Reading Partners" program for students in kindergarten through third grade for four weeks. Students who participate will receive a certificate and prize at the P.A.R.P. assembly at the end of the program. The objectives of this program are:

1. To develop a positive attitude toward reading, and;

2. Development of life long reading habits.

How can your family become involved? You can follow these easy steps:

1. Read and sign the attached contract. Have your child color the picture and return both to school by November 2nd.

2. Post the Calendar Time Sheets on a home bulletin board or refrigerator door.

3. Read with your child 15 minutes a day for 5 days each week beginning November 2nd and ending November 29th. Initial the Calendar Time Sheet each day that you read.

4. Return the bottom portion of the Time Sheet to the classroom teacher on the days that are indicated.

In the event that both parents work or there are extenuating circumstances, another adult may read with your child. For example: a grandparent, aunt, uncle, or adult sibling can be your child's reading partner. A substitute reading partner (other than a parent) should sign his/her name on the coupon.

Sincerely,

Cindy Christopher

Cindy Christopher
Chairperson

LEARNING BEGINS AT HOME — READ TO SOMEONE YOU LOVE!!

112

TULLY ELEMENTARY P.A.R.P.

CONTRACT

I promise to read with my child at least 15 minutes per day, five (5) times a week for four (4) weeks, beginning November 2 and ending November 29, 1992.

_____
Parent's Signature

I promise to read with a parent at least 15 minutes per day, five (5) times a week for four (4) weeks, beginning November 2 and ending November 29, 1992.

_____
Child's Signature

PLEASE RETURN THIS CONTRACT TO YOUR CHILD'S TEACHER BY OCTOBER 30, 1992.

_____
Name of your child's teacher

CALENDAR TIME SHEET

CHILD'S NAME _____
                          Please print

TEACHER _____

GRADE _____

My child and I have taken part in our family reading activity for at least 15 minutes on each of the days initialed below.

_____
Parent's Signature

Week 1

NOV	1	2	3	4	5	6	7

************ RETURN THIS PORTION ON MONDAY, NOVEMBER 9TH ************

. . . .

CALENDAR TIME SHEET

CHILD'S NAME _____
                          Please print

TEACHER _____

GRADE _____

My child and I have taken part in our family reading activity for at least 15 minutes on each of the days initialed below.

_____
Parent's Signature

Week 2

NOV	8	9	10	11	12	13	14

************ RETURN THIS PORTION ON MONDAY, NOVEMBER 16th ************

114

Examples of Nongraded Report Cards

Tully Central School
Tully, N.Y. 13159

Kindergarten
19_____ - 19_____

Pupil _____

Teacher _____

Growth and Development	10	20	30	40
1. Dresses self				
2. Obeys rules				
3. Plays/works with others				
4. Shows consideration for others				
5. Appears self-confident				
6. Adjusts easily to new situations				
7. Is cooperative				
8. Accepts responsibility for own actions				
9. Respects rights & property of others				
10. Controls pencil/scissors well				

Work Habits	10	20	30	40
1. Follows directions				
2. Has good attention span				
3. Completes activities on time				
4. Works well independently				
5. Takes care of materials				
6. Accepts suggestions				
7. Works quietly				
8. Tries to do his/her best				
9. Is a good listener				

Language Development	10	20	30	40
1. Speaks clearly				
2. Expresses ideas well				
3. Takes part in group discussions				

Readiness skills	10	20	30	40
1. Recognizes own name (F=first, L=last)				
2. Identifies capital letters				
3. Identifies lower case letters				
4. Sees likenessess & differences				
5. Shows interest in books/stories				
6. Knows address (street, town, state)				
7. Identifies 8 basic colors				
8. Knows own birthday				
9. Knows phone number				
10. Writes own name (F=first, L=last)				

	10	20	30	40
1. Can count to:	25	50	100	
2. Recognizes numbers to:	10	20	30	
3. Writes numbers 1-10				
4. Identifies basic shapes				
5. Uses counting to find out how many				

Attendance Record	10	20	30	40
Days Absent				
Times Tardy				

Placement 19_____ - 19_____
Promoted/Transferred to Grade _____

Teacher's name _____

_____
Principal's signature

116

Tully Central School
First Grade Progress Report
19__ to 19__

Name_____ Teacher _____

Marking Key: X - Not working on yet   * Denotes modified work

M	V	P	I	H	U
Mastery Learning Complete	Very Good Consistently does well	Progressing Shows Steady Growth	Improving Has shown recent growth	Having difficulty, Needs more time & experience	Unsatisfactory

Reading Readiness / Reading Report	1	2	3	4
Instructional Level (see below)				
Identifies letters of alphabet in random order				
____upper case ____lower case				
Can rhyme words				
Knows consonant sounds				
Knows vowel sounds				
Blends sounds into words				
Knows sight words				
Uses word analysis skills (word endings, contractions, etc.)				

Reading Comprehension				
Recalls details				
Relates main idea				
Can sequence events				
Relates cause and effect				
Reads fluently for meaning				
*READING EFFORT				

Mathematics				
Identifies O △ □ ▭				
Understands the uses of measurement tools				
Recognizes numerals to...				
Writes by 1's				
Writes by 2's				
Writes by 5's				
Writes by 10's				
Knows basic addition facts				
Knows basic subtraction facts				
Understands place values (tens and ones)				
Recognizes coins				
Can tell time ____on hour ____on half hour				
Applies math concepts to problem solving				
*MATH EFFORT				

ATTENDANCE RECORD	1	2	3	4
Days Absent				
Times Tardy				
Illegal Absents				
Illegal Tardy				

Language Development / Listening Report	1	2	3	4
Listens to and comprehends stories read				
Speaks clearly				
Expresses ideas well				
Takes part in group discussions				
*LANGUAGE EFFORT				

Writing				
Expresses ideas in writing __draws pictures__writes letters __words __sentences				
*WRITING EFFORT				

Penmanship				
Demonstrates fine motor coordination				
Is able to form letters correctly				
Is able to space correctly				
Applies skills in daily work				
*PENMANSHIP EFFORT				

Work Habits				
Works well in a large group				
Works well in a small group				
Works well independently and quietly				
Listens to and follows directions				
Completes work on time				
Puts forth best effort				
Uses free time wisely				
Accepts responsibility for learning				

Social Behavior				
Follows rules and routines				
Manages personal belongings				
Respects rights and feelings of others				
Solves own problems				
Accepts responsibility for own actions				

Scott Foresman	Reading Levels
Come Along	Level 1
Friends	Level 2A
Prizes	Level 2B
Colors	Level 2C
Outside My Window	Level 3
Story Clouds	Level 4

Tully Elementary School
Second Grade Progress Report
19___ to 19___

Name_____ Teacher _____

Marking Key: X - Not working on yet   * Denotes modified work

M	V	P	I	H	U
Mastery	Very Good	Progressing	Improving		Unsatisfactory
Learning Complete	Consistently does well	Shows Steady Growth	Has shown recent growth	Having difficulty, Needs more time & experience	

Scott Foresman Reading Levels
  Grade 1: Story Clouds   Level 4
  Grade 2: Under the Moon   Level 5
  Grade 2: What Do I See   Level 6

Attendance

	Legal				Illegal		
Days Absent							
Times Tardy							

READING	1	2	3	4
Instructional Level				
Uses Word Attack Skills				
Knows Sight Words				
Understands Vocabulary at Reading Level				
Self Corrects				
Comprehends What is Read				
Chooses To Read Independently				
Effort				

MATHEMATICS	1	2	3	4
Knows basic addition facts through (9,18)				
Knows basic subtraction facts through (9,18)				
Understands Place Value				
Can identify coins and count coins accurately				
Can tell time to hour, 1/2 hour, minutes				
Regroups				
Understands and uses measurement				
Uses appropriate problem solving strategies				
Understands terms and concepts				
Effort				

SPELLING	1	2	3	4
Learns Weekly Spelling Words				
Retains Spelling for own Writing				
Uses Resources to Spell Words				
Effort				

HANDWRITING	1	2	3	4
Forms Letters Correctly				
Uses Appropriate Spaces				
Neatness In Daily Work				
Effort				

LANGUAGE ARTS	1	2	3	4
Expresses Ideas Clearly				
Writes In Complete Sentences				
Stories are appropriately sequenced				
Uses Correct Capitilization				
Uses Correct Punctuation				
Understands Writing Process				
Effort				

WORK HABITS	1	2	3	4
Works well independently				
Works well with a partner				
Works well with a group				
Completes work on time				
Is organized				
Stays on task				
Listens attentively				
Follows directions				
Volunteers information				
Asks questions when necessary				

SOCIAL SKILLS	1	2	3	4
Follows classroom rules				
Follows school rules				
Plays well with others				
Respects others				
Accepts responsibility				

118

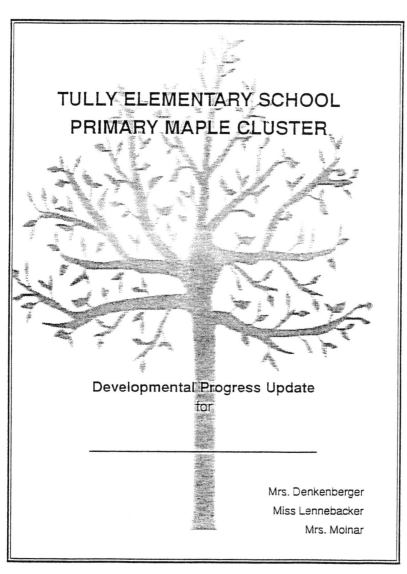

TULLY ELEMENTARY SCHOOL
PRIMARY MAPLE CLUSTER

Developmental Progress Update
for

_____

Mrs. Denkenberger
Miss Lennebacker
Mrs. Molnar

Multiage K–2.

DEVELOPMENT OF SOCIAL SKILLS AND WORK HABITS	Year 1			Year 2			Year 3		
KEY ⊠ = I am successful. ⧄ = I am making progress. □ = I need more time.	Nov. / Dec.	March	June	Nov. / Dec.	March	June	Nov. / Dec.	March	June
Takes responsibility for own actions									
Takes care of and cleans up materials									
Keeps personal materials organized									
Explores and tries new things									
Respects rights and property of others									
Works cooperatively / well with others									
Participates appropriately in learning activities									
Adapts to a variety of learning environments									
Has positive self–concept									
Has positive outlook toward school environment									
Shows interest and initiative									
Completes tasks neatly and accurately									
Exhibits self–control									
Controls voice level to environment									
Works well individually									
Makes responsible choices									
Completes tasks and makes good use of time									
Completes tasks without excessive adult supervision									
Listens attentively									
Follows directions									
Demonstrates an adequate attention span									

READINESS SKILLS	Year 1			Year 2			Year 3		
KEY ⊠ = I am successful. ⧄ = I am making progress. ☐ = I need more time.	Nov. / Dec.	March	June	Nov. / Dec.	March	June	Nov. / Dec.	March	June
PERSONAL INFORMATION									
Knows full name									
Knows address									
Knows telephone number									
Knows birthday									
MOTOR DEVELOPMENT									
Holds pencil and crayon correctly									
Uses scissors correctly									
Manages clothes independently									
READINESS SKILLS FOR READING AND MATHEMATICS									
Prints first and last name									
Prints letters of the alphabet									
Can rhyme words									
Enjoys books									
Uses pictures to help understand a story									
Uses letters / words to accompany illustrations									
Recognizes numerals to 10									
Identifies basic shapes (circle, square, triangle, rectangle)									
Recognizes 8 basic colors									

DEVELOPMENT OF LANGUAGE ARTS	Year 1			Year 2			Year 3		
KEY ⊠ = Experiences independent success. ⊿ = Instruct, prompt and reinforce when appropriate. ▯ = Not applicable at this time.	Nov. / Dec.	March	June	Nov. / Dec.	March	June	Nov. / Dec.	March	June
READING									
Awareness that print has meaning									
Recognizes letters of the alphabet in random order									
Knows letter sounds									
Uses sounds to decode unknown words									
Uses meaning / picture and structural cues									
Retells story or information in own words									
Can summarize									
Discusses main idea, setting, and characters									
Can sequence events of a story									
Reads fluently with expression									
Has adequate sight vocabulary									
Knows when and where to seek help									
SPEAKING / LISTENING									
Expresses ideas clearly									
Participates effectively in class									
Listens and retains important details									

DEVELOPMENT OF LANGUAGE ARTS (cont.)	Year 1			Year 2			Year 3		
KEY ⊠ = Experiences independent success. ⊘ = Instruct, prompt and reinforce when appropriate. ☐ = Not applicable at this time.	Nov. / Dec.	March	June	Nov. / Dec.	March	June	Nov. / Dec.	March	June
PENMANSHIP									
Writes legibly									
Has appropriate spacing									
Forms letters and numerals correctly									
Applies penmanship skills in work									
WRITING / SPELLING									
Content directly relates to topic									
Demonstrates beginning, middle, end									
Writes for a variety of purposes / audiences									
Varies sentence structure									
Spells familiar words correctly									
Writing shows insight and imagination									
Attempts to revise / edit drafts									
Uses capital letters appropriately									
Uses appropriate punctuation at the end of a sentence									
Knows when and where to seek help									
WRITING STAGE (Dated when evident)									
Draws pictures									
Writes letters									
Writes words									
Writes sentences									
Writes paragraphs									

DEVELOPMENT OF MATHEMATICS	Year 1			Year 2			Year 3		
KEY ⊠ = Experiences independent success. ▨ = Instruct, prompt and reinforce when appropriate. ▯ = Not applicable at this time.	Nov. / Dec.	March	June	Nov. / Dec.	March	June	Nov. / Dec.	March	June
Counts to 100 (or beyond)									
Counts by 2's to 100									
Counts by 5's to 100									
Counts by 10's to 100									
Copies, extends, and creates patterns									
Matches numerals to number sets									
Identifies geometric shapes									
Understands place value to 10									
Understands place value to 100									
Understands place value to 1000									
Adds and subtracts with manipulatives									
Knows basic addition facts to 10									
Knows basic addition facts to 20									
Knows basic subtraction facts to 10									
Knows basic subtraction facts to 20									
Understands two–digit addition without regrouping									
Understands two–digit addition with regrouping									
Understands two–digit subtraction without regrouping									
Understands two–digit subtraction with regrouping									

DEVELOPMENT OF MATHEMATICS (cont.)		Year 1			Year 2			Year 3		
KEY ⊠ = Experiences independent success. ▨ = Instruct, prompt and reinforce when appropriate. ▢ = Not applicable at this time.		Nov. / Dec.	March	June	Nov. / Dec.	March	June	Nov. / Dec.	March	June
Tells time to:	hour									
	half hour									
	five minute intervals									
Understands fractions:	1/2									
	1/3									
	1/4									
Counts money:	1¢, 5¢, 10¢									
	25¢, 50¢, $1.00									
Has measurement awareness										
Has graphing awareness										
Can read a calendar										

Primary Maple Cluster

Developmental Progress Update

Narrative for _____

Nov./Dec.   Mar.   June   Year_____   Homeroom: Lennebacker
                                                                        Denkenberger
                                                                        Molnar

What are some signs of my success during the last marking period?

What will I be concentrating on during the next marking period?

What can I do at home to practice or improve?

126

GRADES 1-3
TULLY ELEMENTARY SCHOOL SPECIAL SUBJECT PROGRESS REPORT

STUDENT'S NAME_____GRADE_____SCHOOL YEAR_____.

S = Satisfactory
U = Unsatisfactory | ART TEACHER |_____

COMMENTS: 20 Weeks   GRADE_____   COMMENTS: 40 Weeks   GRADE_____

S = Satisfactory
U = Unsatisfactory   Your child is learning to sing, play, write, and
                            hear music. He (she) is growing in these
                            musical understandings through participation in
                            musical activities within the classroom.

| GENERAL MUSIC TEACHER |_____

20 Weeks: 40 Weeks:

_____ Participation   _____ Participation

_____ Effort   _____ Effort

_____ Behavior   _____ Behavior

_____ Overall Performance   _____ Overall Performance

S = Satisfactory   Physical Education helps children develop fitness, become independent learners
U = Unsatisfactory   and develop social skills by interacting with other students.

| P.E. TEACHER |_____

20 Weeks: 40 Weeks:

_____ Skill Performance   _____ Skill Performance

_____ Effort   _____ Effort

_____ Behavior   _____ Behavior

_____ Responsibility (Proper attire)   _____ Responsibility (Proper attire)

_____ Sportsmanship   _____ Sportsmanship

127

Rubric Examples

Jane Panzarella, a fifth grade teacher, uses many different rubrics in her classroom. She finds they help her to be much more precise in what she expects and students are able to be more focused because they know her expectations and requirements ahead of time.

On page 130 is a rubric Jane uses when having students design a map from home to school. Not only do the students check to make sure they put the correct things on, but their peer and the teacher check as well. On page 131 is a rubric for designing a regional map of the United States.

When reading novels, Jane uses rubrics for small group discussions. The top part of the contract on page 132 is decided on by the group and then taken home to be finished by each member. The next day each group completes the discussion result sheets found on pages 133 and 134. On page 135 the recorder fills out the rubric at the end of the session. The teacher then looks over the work and completes the rubric.

The last example of a rubric came from second grade teachers, Cindy Denkenberger and Kathy Rogers. They use a spelling task rubric weekly in each of their classrooms.

Map from Home to School

Name: _____   Date: _____

Key: Y=yes   NY=not yet

	self	peer	teacher
title			
north pointer			
names of roads, intersections			
landmarks (churches, stores, parks, lakes, etc.)			
decide upon a scale with parent or teacher input			
map key			
rough draft			

Regional Map of United States

Group Study of_____

Group Name_____

		self yes	self not yet	peer yes	peer not yet	teacher yes	teacher not yet
M A P	political, physical, climatic,						
	population, or product						
	important cities, countries, states listed						
	colored, labeled clearly						
	key						
I N F O R M A T I O N	economy($) -examples of possible jobs						
	natural resources--use graph, chart or map						
	historical facts--paragraph form, chronological order						
	climate--examples of weather --how related to latitude						
	people --ancestors came from...... and						
	culture--give examples of traditions, holidays, etc.						
	landforms--classify different types with where they are						
	major cities--where they are why it is important						
	natural regions--list the relationships within each area						
	interesting facts--classify some facts about the area						

Contract

I promise to read _____ tonight. I

also promise to write 2 questions and 4 vocabulary words

for each chapter I read. Signature:_____

Chapter_____

Questions: 1. _____

_____

2. _____

_____

Vocabulary: 1. _____   page _____

2. _____   page _____

3. _____   page _____

4. _____   page_____

Chapter_____

Questions: 1. _____

_____

2. _____

_____

Vocabulary: 1. _____   page _____

2. _____   page _____

3. _____   page _____

4. _____   page_____

Discussion Results

During group discussion you must talk about the chapters you read in preparation for the day's discussion. Each person in the group will be responsible, on a rotating basis, for being the recorder for the group. The recorder will listen to the discussion and record the most important information discussed that day. The recorder has overnight to fill in the discussion chart and make sure it is placed in the group's folder. The information must be presented in good English and must be legible (cursive is required).

Recorder's Name _____

The event we enjoyed or talked about the most is: (this event may be funny, scary, important, dramatic, suspenceful, action packed, etc.)_____

_____

_____

_____

_____

_____

_____

_____

The best question and the answer to that question is:
_____ wrote the question recorded below.

_____

_____

_____

_____

_____

_____

Vocabulary words discussed with a sentence for each to show meaning:

1. _____
   _____
   _____
2. _____
   _____
   _____
3. _____
   _____
   _____
4. _____
   _____
   _____
5. _____
   _____
   _____

I have recorded the information from our book discussion on _____ to the best of my ability.
Signature of recorder: _____

Novel Reading Tasks Rubric
Week 1,2,3,4
(circle one)

Code: A=all, S=some, +=well done, -=needs improvement

	Recorder			Teacher		
	Day 1	Day 2	Day3	Day 1	Day 2	Day 3
Chapters were read as agreed upon						
Questions & vocab. were completed for each chapter						
Participation in group						
Materials are organized in folder						

Comments:

Student recorder: _____

_____

_____

Teacher: _____

_____

135

Spelling Tasks

Name _____

	Week					
Monday — Add new words to list.						
Write in Q-W book.						
Copy list for home.						
Tuesday Copy words 5X each.						
Wednesday Use words in sentences.						
Thursday Do special activities.						
Friday Do test and hand in.						
Score:						
Teacher's comments:						

Addresses of Programs

Addresses of people to contact for further information concerning some of the programs mentioned throughout the book.

Doughnuts for Dads/Muffins for Mom
  Jackson-Keller Elementary School
  Alicia Thomas, Principal
  1601 Jackson-Keller
  San Antonio, Texas 78213
  210-525-0971

Homework Hotline
  The Syracuse Newspapers
  Stan Linhorst/John Mariani
  Clinton Square
  P.O. Box 4818
  Syracuse, NY 13221-4818
  315-470-2158   Fax: 315-470-6080

Lesson Line
  First Tennessee Bank
  Leslie Lee
  P.O. Box 84
  Memphis, TN 38101

Los Angeles Parent Institute for Quality Education
  Margie Martinez-Madrigal, Executive Program Director
  3370 San Fernando Rd., Unit 105
  Los Angeles, California 90065
  213-255-2575   Fax: 213-255-5120

Parent Resource Room
  Molholm Elementary School
  6000 W. 9th Ave.
  Lakewood, CO 80214
  303-237-9503

Parent's Group
  Dann C. Byck Elementary School
  Stephany Hoover
  2328 Cedar Street
  Louisville, Kentucky 40212
  502-485-8221

P.A.R.P.
  NYS P.T.A.
  119 Washington Ave.
  Albany, NY 12210

Report Cards for Parents
  Frederick Douglass Elementary School
  226 N. Jim Miller
  Dallas, Texas 75217
  214-309-7180

The Community Parent Education Program (COPE)
  Charles E. Cunningham
  Rebecca Bremner
  Margaret Secord-Gilbert
  Chedoke-McMaster Hospitals

The National PTA
  700 North Rush Street
  Chicago, IL 60611
  312-787-8342

Anderson, R. H. and B. V. Paven. 1993. *Nongradedness—Helping It to Happen*. Lancaster, PA: Technomic Publishing Co., Inc.

Archbald, D. A. 1991. *Authentic Assessment: What It Means and How It Can Help Schools*. Madison, WI: National Center for Effective Schools Research and Development.

Brandt, R. S. 1992. *Performance Assessment*. Association for Supervision and Curriculum Development.

Burke, K. 1994. *How to Assess Authentic Learning*. Illinois: Skylight Publishing, Inc.

Cohen, D. L. 1990. "A Look at Multiage Classrooms," *Education Digest,* 55(9):20–23.

Cohen, E. G. *Designing Groupwork*. New York: Teacher's College Press.

Gaustad, J. 1992. "Making the Transition from Graded to Nongraded Primary Education," *OSSC Bulletin*.

Herman, J. L., P. R. Aschbacher and L. Winters. 1992. "A Practical Guide to Alternative Assessment." Association for Supervision and Curriculum Development.

Hunter, M. 1992. *How to Change to a Nongraded School*. Alexandria, VA: Association for Supervision and Curriculum Development.

Johnson, D. W. and R. T. Johnson. *Learning Together and Alone*. Englewood Cliffs, NJ: Prentice-Hall.

Johnson, D. W., R. T. Johnson and E. J. Holubec. *Structuring Cooperative Learning: Lesson Plans for Teachers*. Edina, MN: Interaction Book Co.

Kagan, S. *Cooperative Learning: The Structured Approach*. San Juan Capistrano: Resources for Teachers.

Lodish, R. 1992. *The Pros and Cons of Mixed-Age Grouping*. Alexandria, VA: National Association of Elementary School Principals.

Paven, B. N. 1992. "The Benefits of Nongraded Schools," *Educational Leadership,* 50(2):22–25.

Surbeck, E. 1992. "Multiage Programs in Primary Grades: Are They Educationally Appropriate?" *Childhood Educ.,* 69(1):3–4.

CINDY CHRISTOPHER GRADUATED in 1980 with a B.S. in elementary education from the State University of New York at Cortland and in 1990 with an M.S. She currently teaches third grade in Tully, New York and conducts workshops for teachers throughout the state. Cindy wrote her first book in 1992 titled, *Nuts and Bolts Survival Guide for Teachers.* She also writes devotional material for *The Secret Place,* and has written a nonpublished children's book. She enjoys camping, reading, biking, singing, and sewing quilts. She sells crafts and Amish furniture in her spare time. Cindy is also very involved in the First Baptist Church of Homer, New York, and leads a bible study in her home.

Dear Educator,

Thank you for purchasing this book. I would love to hear from you if you have any new ideas or programs that involve, inform, or include parents. Please send responses to:

Cindy J. Christopher
P.O. Box 75
Little York, New York 13087-0075